# Tableau Prep Cookbook

Use Tableau Prep to clean, combine, and transform your data for analysis

**Hendrik Kleine**

BIRMINGHAM—MUMBAI

# Tableau Prep Cookbook

**Group Product Manager**: Kunal Parikh
**Publishing Product Manager**: Sunith Shetty
**Senior Editor**: David Sugarman
**Content Development Editor**: Nathanya Dias
**Technical Editor**: Sonam Pandey
**Copy Editor**: Safis Editing
**Project Coordinator**: Aishwarya Mohan
**Proofreader**: Safis Editing
**Indexer**: Priyanka Dhadke
**Production Designer**: Aparna Bhagat

First published: March 2021

Production reference: 1170221

Published by Packt Publishing Ltd.
Livery Place
35 Livery Street
Birmingham
B3 2PB, UK.

ISBN 978-1-80056-376-6

www.packt.com

# Contributors

## About the author

**Hendrik Kleine** is an advanced analytics leader with 15 years of experience in the analytics space, including in data architecture, engineering, and visualization. He specializes in translating vast amounts of data into easy-to-understand visual communications that provide actionable intelligence. He is an avid innovator and a listed author of multiple data-related inventions. Before COVID-19, he was a speaker at the most recent Tableau conference in San Francisco.

*I want to thank the people who have motivated, supported, and inspired me, especially my wife, Kinga, and our beautiful children, Holden and Fallon.*

# About the reviewers

**Fabian Peri's** interest in decision analysis started after joining his first fantasy basketball league in 2006. His love for data analysis led him to pursue an MBA in information systems at the University of Tulsa, and then an MSc in predictive analytics from Northwestern University. Since graduating, he has primarily worked in risk analysis and management for companies such as Amazon, GE Capital, and Wells Fargo. He is currently focused on using visualization to explore and interpret vast quantities of data.

**Vicente Ruben** is a data professional with more than a decade of experience in big data analytics. His expertise comprises architecture design and the development and implementation of business intelligence and data warehouse environments at scale. Vicente Ruben has implemented big data solutions for several Fortune 20 companies and currently leads data engineering solutions at one of the world's largest healthcare companies. He has expertise in a wide range of technologies, ranging from relational databases such as SQL Server and business intelligence suites such as the Microsoft stack (Azure and SQL Server) to NoSQL databases such as MongoDB and CouchBase and cloud services such as Azure and AWS.

# Table of Contents

## Preface

## 1

## Getting Started with Tableau Prep

## 2

## Extract and Load Processes

# 3

# Cleaning Transformations

# 4

# Data Aggregation

# 5

# Combining Data

# 6

# Pivoting Data

# 7

# Creating Powerful Calculations

# 8
## Data Science in Tableau Prep Builder

# 9
## Creating Prep Flows in Various Business Scenarios

## Other Books You May Enjoy

## Index

# Preface

Tableau Prep is a relatively new tool for data preparation. It is designed around a core set of data preparation capabilities such as cleaning, joining, and aggregating data in preparation for analysis. Tableau Prep leverages a modern and intuitive user interface to allow you to create new data flows quickly and efficiently in a fraction of the time it may have taken in traditional, complex ETL tools.

In this book, you'll learn how to perform key actions in Tableau Prep, in order to build your own data flow, from data ingestion, cleaning, and transforming, to creating an output for data analysis.

## Who this book is for

This book is for business intelligence professionals, data analysts, and Tableau users looking to learn Tableau Prep essentials and create data pipelines or ETL processes using it. Basic knowledge of data management will be beneficial to understand the concepts covered in this Tableau Prep cookbook more effectively.

## What this book covers

*Chapter 1*, *Getting Started with Tableau Prep*, runs through the various use cases in which you can employ Tableau Prep as a tool for data analysis.

*Chapter 2*, *Extract and Load Processes*, explains how to connect to various data source types and write your output to different destinations.

*Chapter 3*, *Cleaning Transformations*, covers how to apply cleaning operations to your dataset, including filtering, validation, and splitting columns.

*Chapter 4*, *Data Aggregation*, looks at how to aggregate data using aggregation and grouping functions.

*Chapter 5*, *Combining Data*, addresses how to join various disparate datasets using join and union tools.

*Chapter 6, Pivoting Data,* looks at how to pivot the orientation of your data from columns to rows and vice versa.

*Chapter 7, Creating Powerful Calculations,* explains how to add calculated fields to your dataset.

*Chapter 8, Data Science in Tableau Prep Builder,* covers how to add R or Python code to your Tableau Prep data flow.

*Chapter 9, Creating Prep Flows in Various Business Scenarios,* lets you practice a full end-to-end flow creation using a variety of methods discussed in this book.

# To get the most out of this book

You will need to have Tableau Prep Builder installed on your desktop, preferably the most recent version. All exercises in this book have been tested with version 2021.1 on Windows 10 and macOS Big Sur.

| Software Covered | OS Requirements |
|---|---|
| Tableau Prep Builder | Windows or macOS |
| Python 3.8.7 | Windows or macOS |
| R | Windows or macOS |
| RStudio | Windows or macOS |

Note that Python, R, and RStudio are only required to complete the exercises in *Chapter 8, Data Science in Tableau Prep Builder.*

**If you are using the digital version of this book, we advise you to type the code yourself or access the code via the GitHub repository (link available in the next section). Doing so will help you avoid any potential errors related to the copying and pasting of code.**

# Download the example code files

You can download the example code files for this book from GitHub at `https://github.com/PacktPublishing/Tableau-Prep-Cookbook`. In case there's an update to the code, it will be updated on the existing GitHub repository.

We also have other code bundles from our rich catalog of books and videos available at `https://github.com/PacktPublishing/`. Check them out!

# Download the color images

We also provide a PDF file that has color images of the screenshots/diagrams used in this book. You can download it here: `https://static.packt-cdn.com/downloads/9781800563766_ColorImages.pdf`.

# Conventions used

There are a number of text conventions used throughout this book.

`Code in text`: Indicates code words in text, database table names, folder names, filenames, file extensions, pathnames, dummy URLs, user input, and Twitter handles. Here is an example: "Open the Tableau Prep `Superstore` flow to follow along with the steps outlined."

A block of code is set as follows:

```
IF [Segment] = "Consumer" THEN TRUE ELSE FALSE END
```

**Bold**: Indicates a new term, an important word, or words that you see onscreen. For example, words in menus or dialog boxes appear in the text like this. Here is an example: "If you do have a product key, you can always add it via the **Help** menu under **Manage Product Keys**."

> **Tips or important notes**
> Appear like this.

# Get in touch

Feedback from our readers is always welcome.

**General feedback**: If you have questions about any aspect of this book, mention the book title in the subject of your message and email us at `customercare@packtpub.com`.

**Errata**: Although we have taken every care to ensure the accuracy of our content, mistakes do happen. If you have found a mistake in this book, we would be grateful if you would report this to us. Please visit `www.packtpub.com/support/errata`, selecting your book, clicking on the Errata Submission Form link, and entering the details.

**Piracy**: If you come across any illegal copies of our works in any form on the Internet, we would be grateful if you would provide us with the location address or website name. Please contact us at `copyright@packt.com` with a link to the material.

**If you are interested in becoming an author**: If there is a topic that you have expertise in and you are interested in either writing or contributing to a book, please visit authors.packtpub.com.

# Reviews

Please leave a review. Once you have read and used this book, why not leave a review on the site that you purchased it from? Potential readers can then see and use your unbiased opinion to make purchase decisions, we at Packt can understand what you think about our products, and our authors can see your feedback on their book. Thank you!

For more information about Packt, please visit packt.com.

# 1
# Getting Started with Tableau Prep

**Tableau Prep Builder** is an exciting new platform to develop data pipelines to transform your data for reporting and analytics purposes.

In this chapter, you will come to understand how we think about data preparation from the perspective of Tableau Prep Builder. You will learn about the different use cases you may employ Tableau Prep for, be it ad hoc data analysis, creating a dataset for a BI tool, or specifically for **Tableau Desktop**.

In this chapter, we will cover the following recipes:

- Installing Tableau Prep Builder
- Checking out the user interface
- Using Tableau Prep for ad hoc data analysis
- Preparing data for generic BI tools
- Preparing data for Tableau Desktop ad hoc analysis

# Technical requirements

To follow along with the recipes in this chapter, you need to have **Tableau Prep Builder** installed, and **Tableau Desktop**. In the first recipe, we'll walk through the details of installing Tableau Prep Builder.

# Installing Tableau Prep Builder

In this recipe, you'll install **Tableau Prep Builder**. We'll download the software, perform the installation, and open **Tableau Prep Builder** for the first time.

## Getting ready

To enjoy the many benefits of Tableau Prep Builder, you need a license key. Typically, this would be issued by your administrator. Alternatively, you may have purchased a license yourself at `https://buy.tableau.com/`.

If you do not have a license key, Tableau offers a free trial so you can start right away.

As with all recipes in this book, the installation is performed on an Apple MacBook running **macOS Big Sur**. The steps are nearly identical on **Windows** machines and you can follow along on either operating system.

## How to do it...

Ensure you're connected to the internet and have your favorite browser open:

1. Navigate to `https://www.tableau.com/products/prep/download`, enter your business email, and click **START FREE TRIAL**:

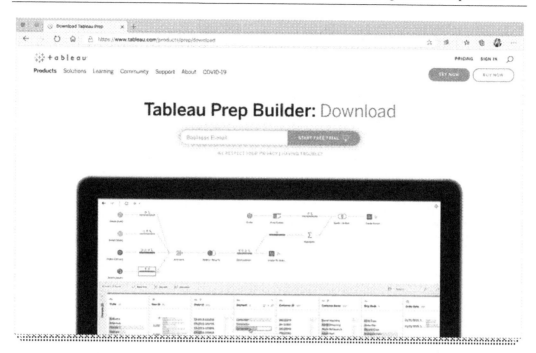

Figure 1.1 – Tableau Prep Builder download site

2.  The installer file should start downloading in a few seconds. Wait until the download has been completed, then proceed to open it. On the first step, click **Continue**.

3.  Review the license agreement and when ready, select **Continue**.

4.  Next, the installer will confirm the installation destination. In most cases, the default location should work. However, you may customize it at this time. When done, click **Install** to continue.

5.  The installer may prompt you for your password. This is normal. Enter your password and click **Install Software** to continue.

6.  When the installation has completed, click **Close**.

7.  You won't be needing the installer file after this, so you may safely delete it. Select **Move to Bin** to do so now.

8.  With the installation completed, you may now open **Tableau Prep Builder** for the first time. Your trial will automatically be activated without the need for a product key. If you do have a product key, you can always add it via the **Help** menu under **Manage Product Keys**.

You're now ready to start using **Tableau Prep Builder** with the recipes in this book.

## How it works...

Tableau Prep Builder is updated frequently, and you may expect new features, enhancements, and bug fixes at a regular cadence. Once you have installed a version, as in this recipe, Tableau Prep Builder will always notify you upon startup if a more recent version is available, along with a link to the download page.

# Checking out the user interface

Tableau has taken great care in creating an interface that is intuitive and easy to understand. Perhaps best of all, it has quite a few similarities to the manner in which things are laid out in Tableau Desktop. So, if you are familiar with Tableau Desktop, you should feel right at home.

In this recipe, we will take a brief tour of the Tableau Prep user interface.

## Getting ready

**Tableau Prep** provides what we need right out of the box. That includes data connectors, sample flows, training resources, and community updates. We'll walk through these step by step. This knowledge is foundational to all recipes.

## How to do it...

Open Tableau Prep:

1.  When you open **Tableau Prep Builder**, you're presented with the home screen. From here, you can take a number of actions, which we'll cover briefly:

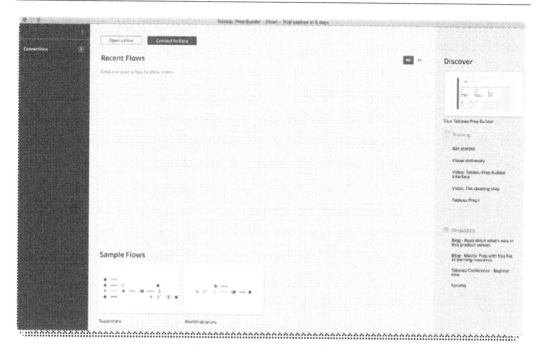

Figure 1.2 – Tableau Prep Builder home page

In Tableau Prep, a **flow** is what we call a data pipeline. If you've used other software in the past, you may have referred to a pipeline as an **Extract, Transform, and Load (ETL)** process, **workflow**, or **data pipeline**.

It's easy to start a new flow, simply by creating a data connection. To get started, click the blue **Connect to Data** button to expand the data connection options:

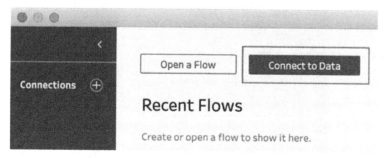

Figure 1.3 – Starting a new flow

From here, select your connection type, and that will complete the creation of a new flow:

Figure 1.4 – Selecting a data connection type

In *Chapter 2, Extract and Load Processes*, we'll cover the configuration of various data connections in detail.

2.  At the bottom of the home page, you'll notice two example flows provided by Tableau:

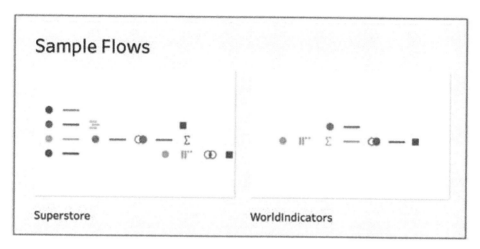

Figure 1.5 – Preinstalled sample flows

Both these flows use the sample `Superstore` and `WorldIndicators` data that is delivered with the Tableau Desktop application as well, so you may be familiar with this data already.

These example flows can be opened with one click and run locally. They're excellent for testing out quick actions and recipes learned in this book, without the need for you to create a new flow from scratch. Personally, I've become so accustomed to this, I typically try something out in an example workflow quickly, and then move on to my own flow and implement the action there when I'm confident it'll work.

3.   To the right side of the home screen, you'll find the **Discover** pane:

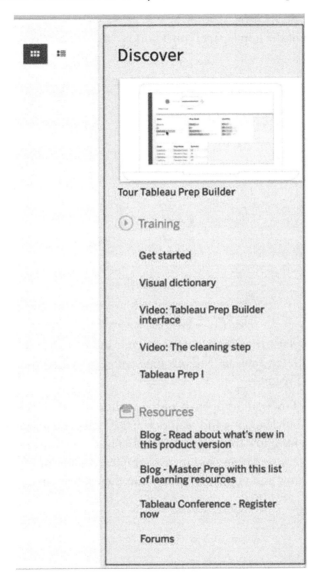

Figure 1.6 – Discover pane

The **Discover** pane has two sections that are always visible, **Training** and **Resources**. **Training** includes links to training materials authored by the Tableau team, while **Resources** includes links to Tableau blogs and user community forums.

These links update over time, so it's great to glance at this pane every time you open Tableau Prep, to make sure you're up to date on the latest developments.

4. There are two ways to open flows. Firstly, you can use the **Open a Flow** button at the top of the home screen.

The second, one-click approach is to select a flow from the **Recent Flows** section. This section will automatically update based on your activity, with the latest flow accessed being the first one listed:

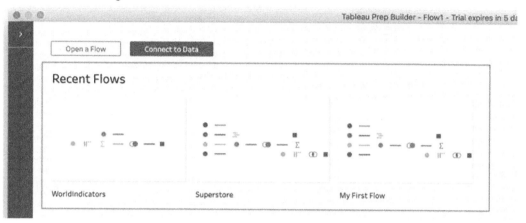

Figure 1.7 – Quick access to Recent Flows

5. Click the **Superstore** flow in the **Recent Flows** section to view a flow in the flow builder interface, which shows you the data input, transformations, and output steps in a single overview:

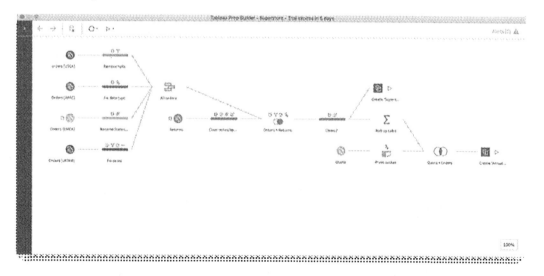

Figure 1.8 – Flow builder interface

6. A key feature of the flow interface is pausing data updates, which you can enable and disable with a single click in the top action bar:

Figure 1.9 – Pausing data updates

7. When data updates are paused, Tableau Prep Builder does not validate all the changes you are making instantly. As a result, you get increased performance. However, some features that require a data preview will be disabled until you resume data updates:

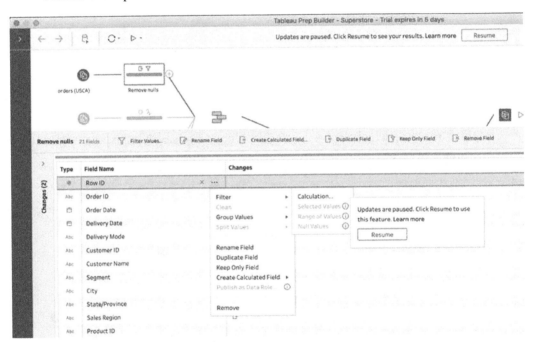

Figure 1.10 – Some features are disabled when data updates are paused

8. Next to the **Pause Data Updates** icon, you'll find the **Data Refresh** button. This comes in handy when you are actively working on a flow and you are expecting changes to your data inputs at the same time. For example, a column may have been added to a data input since you opened the flow. In that case, you'll need to refresh the input to ensure the column becomes visible to Tableau Prep:

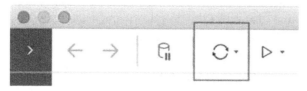

Figure 1.11 – Refreshing all data inputs

9. You can click the button itself to simultaneously update all inputs. Alternatively, open the dropdown to select a single input to update:

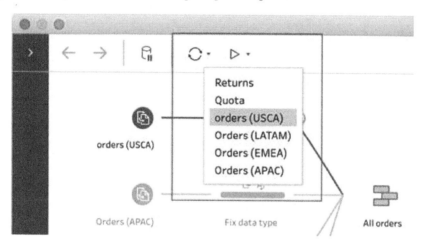

Figure 1.12 – Refreshing specific data inputs

10. The play button in the action bar will run your workflow and produce all outputs with a single click:

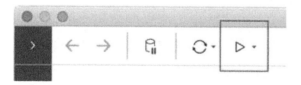

Figure 1.13 – Running an entire data flow

11. However, you may also select the dropdown and select a specific output to be generated only. This could significantly improve the flow runtime, a great benefit during development and testing:

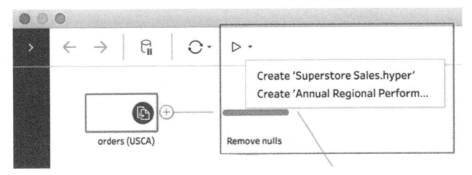

Figure 1.14 – Running a specific data output only

You're now familiar with the foundational elements that make up the **Tableau Prep Builder** user interface and can start building flows using your data.

## How it works...

Simply put, Tableau Prep Builder works by ingesting data from a source to your local machine and processes it there whenever you make updates to a flow, in real time. To stay performant, Tableau Prep Builder automatically takes a sample of your data inputs only during this process. When you execute an entire flow, only then will the full data input be processed, and so this may take longer than previewing data in real time. In *Chapter 2, Extract and Load Processes*, there is a recipe to manage the sampling size and method used by Tableau Prep.

# Using Tableau Prep for ad hoc data analysis

In this recipe, you'll learn how to leverage Tableau Prep Builder to perform ad hoc data analysis. In most scenarios, getting insights from your data would involve the creation of a data pipeline and then connecting a data visualization tool to the output of that pipeline to perform your analysis. However, with Tableau Prep Builder, you can perform basic ad hoc analysis on your data from within the tool itself.

# Getting ready

Open the Tableau Prep **Superstore** flow to follow along with the steps outlined.

# How to do it...

Ad hoc analysis typically starts with a business question to be answered with the use of your data. Let's assume the question posed for the **Superstore** data is: *Which is the top category of products that consumers order with same-day delivery?*

Following these steps, you'll be able to use Tableau Prep to answer this question without the need for additional reporting tools:

1.  In Tableau Prep Builder, select the **All orders** step:

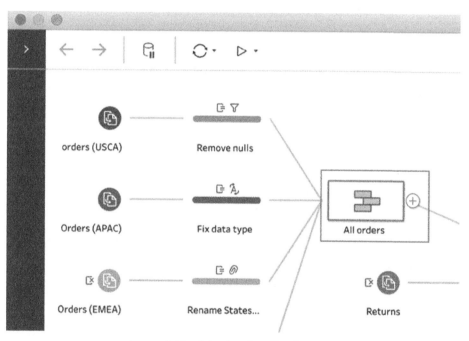

Figure 1.15 – Selecting the All orders step

2.  Whenever we select a step in Tableau Prep, the bottom pane will become visible. The pane will leverage data as it is at the time of the step being selected. In our case, this will be the state of the data after having passed through the **All orders** step:

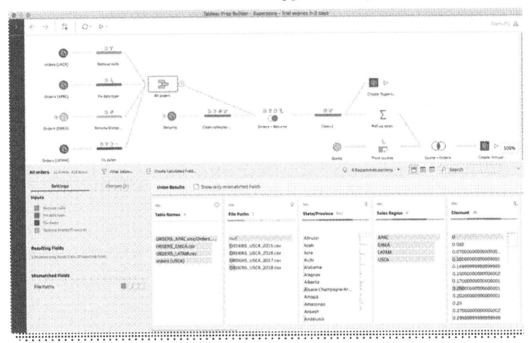

Figure 1.16 – The bottom pane offers many additional options

3.  First, let's reduce the dataset to consumers only. To do this, scroll horizontally through the columns in the results pane until you find the **Segment** column. From the three available values, **Consumer**, **Corporate**, and **Home Office**, right-click **Consumer**. From the context menu, select **Keep Only**:

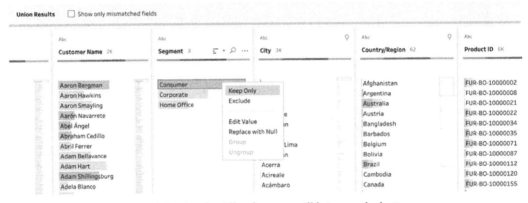

Figure 1.17 – Selecting the All orders step will bring up the bottom pane

Tableau Prep will instantly apply the filter and show you the data preview excluding any segments that are not **Consumer**.

4. Next, locate the **Delivery Mode** field. We could perform the method of filtering as in the previous step. However, an alternate method ideally suited to quick exploratory analysis is using **highlights**. Highlights instantly mark data related to the selected value in the results pane, in a shade of blue. Go ahead and left-click **Same Day** delivery mode.

5. Next, locate the **Category** column and sort its values by descending order:

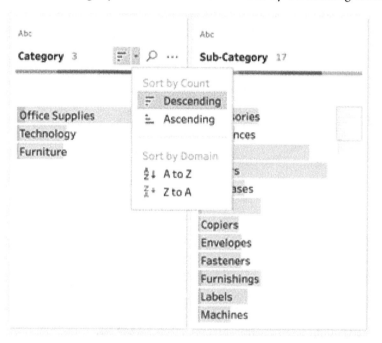

Figure 1.18 – Instantly sort data in Tableau Prep Builder

6.   Now, we can clearly see the top category for consumers' orders with same-day shipping is **Office Supplies**, which is the answer to the business question posed. We can get additional information by hovering over the item and see that 707 rows, or 5% of consumer orders, fall into this category:

Figure 1.19 – Instant category details

With these steps, you've quickly performed ad hoc analysis on the **Superstore** data and identified the top product category for consumers who placed orders with the same-day shipping delivery mode.

## How it works...

Using Tableau Prep Builder, we've quickly performed exploratory data analysis without the need to run our flow or create new outputs. Doing so provides great value not only in terms of a fast turnaround but also in keeping your data landscape clean by avoiding the creation of new data sources (outputs) for simple analysis.

When you perform analysis in this fashion, Tableau Prep instantly runs the required actions in the background to give you the results. In the **Superstore** example flow, this is fairly quick. However, on large datasets, this may take more time. Tableau Prep will show a progress indicator in the top-right corner when performing such background actions:

Figure 1.20 – Background actions

In this recipe, you've learned how to quickly perform ad hoc data analysis in Tableau Prep without the need to export your data for analysis in a downstream application.

# Preparing data for generic BI tools

In this recipe, you'll learn how to use Tableau Prep to generate outputs for consumption by a variety of **Business Intelligence** (**BI**) tools. Specifically, we'll write a single output, from a flow with multiple outputs, to a CSV file. At the time of writing, output to CSV is the only non-Tableau proprietary format supported by Tableau Prep. Future releases of Tableau Prep will see the introduction of output to databases.

## Getting ready

Open the Tableau Prep **Superstore** flow to follow along with the steps outlined.

## How to do it...

In the steps that follow, we'll create an output that is suitable for consumption by data visualization and BI tools other than Tableau Desktop:

1.  Examine the output steps in the **Superstore** flow by clicking either output. In the bottom pane, notice how **Output type** is set to **Tableau Data Extract (.hyper)**. This is the default output format for any output step added to a flow:

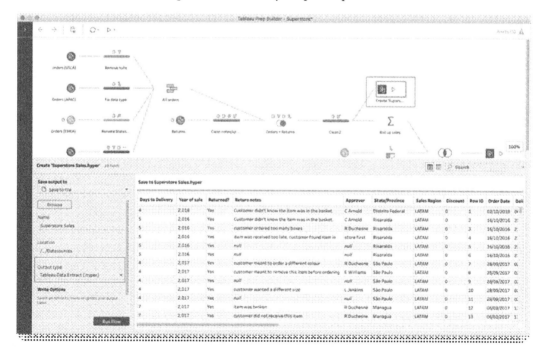

Figure 1.21 – Tableau Prep defaults outputs to .hyper extracts

2.  Since the `.hyper` extract is a proprietary format, it cannot be opened by other applications for further analysis. However, we can change the output type to CSV. CSV outputs are compatible with most leading BI tools and spreadsheet applications:

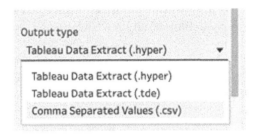

Figure 1.22 – Changing the output type

3.  Once you have an output configured, run just the output that you need to open in the BI tool. If you're using the **Superstore** sample flow, select the Create '**Superstore Sales.csv**' output step and click on the play button within the step. This will ensure the flow only generates this one output, rather than all outputs in the flow:

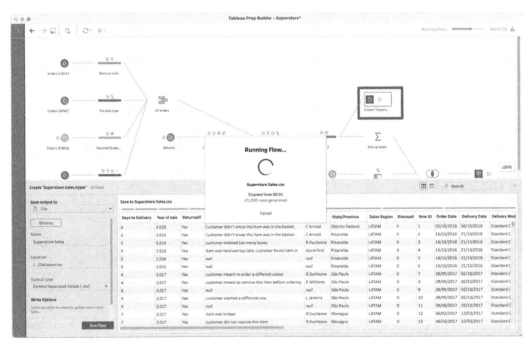

Figure 1.23 – Running a single output

4.  Finally, open the CSV file in the tool of your choice for further analysis. You can keep both Tableau Prep and the analysis application open and, if needed, tweak your flow and run the output again to update the saved CSV file:

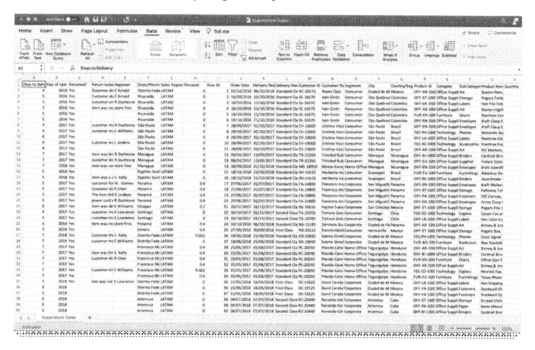

Figure 1.24 – CSV output in Microsoft Excel

You've now successfully completed this recipe and are able to export data to CSV so that you may utilize the transformed dataset in a BI application.

## How it works...

Using the preceding steps, Tableau Prep Builder generates a generic CSV file that can be opened by most popular BI and spreadsheet applications. The benefit of this is that you are free to leverage any tool of your choice and are not locked into any particular ecosystem.

Using Tableau Prep to run distinct outputs separately is a great feature for ad hoc analysis, as you do not need to refresh your entire output every time.

# Preparing data for Tableau Desktop ad hoc analysis

In this recipe, you'll learn how to use Tableau Prep to generate a Tableau Desktop workbook at any point in your flow, to perform further analysis on that data.

Similar to the third recipe, *Using Tableau Prep for ad hoc data analysis*, we'll find the answer to the question posed for the **Superstore** data: *Which is the top category of products that consumers order with same-day delivery?* However, this time, we'll get the answer in Tableau Desktop instead.

## Getting ready

Open the Tableau Prep **Superstore** flow to follow along with the steps outlined. Ensure that Tableau Desktop is installed.

## How to do it...

In the steps that follow, we'll produce a temporary **hyper extract** that will allow us to perform quick ad hoc analysis in Tableau Desktop:

1.  To perform quick ad hoc analysis with a dataset in Tableau Desktop, you can click any step (excluding input and output steps) and select **Preview in Tableau Desktop**. Go ahead and select the **UNION** step, then select **Preview in Tableau Desktop**:

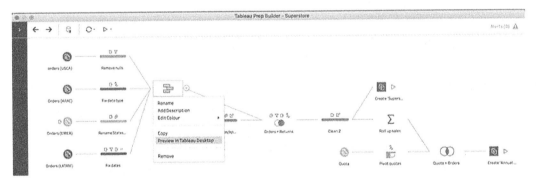

Figure 1.25 – Preview data at any time in Tableau Desktop

2. Within moments, Tableau Desktop will start automatically and open a new workbook connected to the data from the step we selected in the flow:

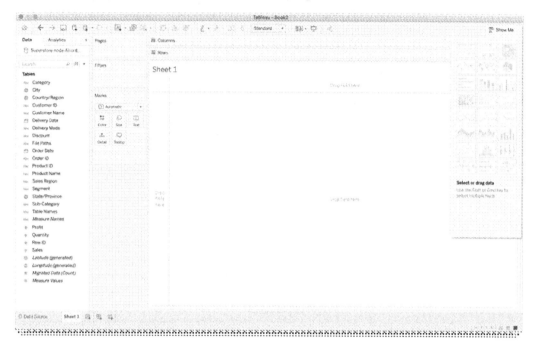

Figure 1.26 – Tableau Desktop workbook automatically created by Tableau Prep

3.  From here, you can perform the typical analysis you'd perform in Tableau Desktop. Add a **Segment** filter for **Consumer**, a **Delivery Mode** filter for **Same Day**, and create a bar chart using the **Category** dimension and the **Migrated Data (Count)** measure, as shown in the following screenshot:

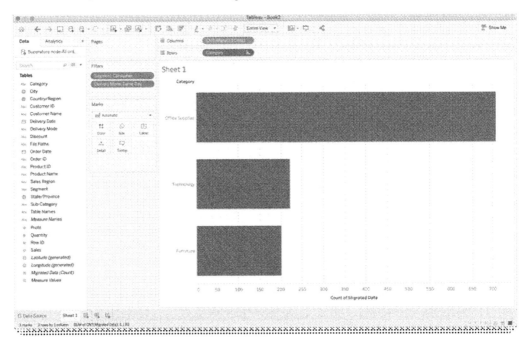

Figure 1.27 – Ad hoc analysis in Tableau Desktop

And with this, we've found the answer to our question. **Office Supplies** is the product category for which consumers most often leverage same-day shipping.

## How it works...

When leveraging the **Preview in Tableau Desktop** functionality, Tableau Prep automatically creates a temporary `.hyper` extract and connects that to a new Tableau workbook. This is ideal for quickly visualizing your data at any point in the data flow, whether that is for exploratory analysis or simply verifying that your flow works as expected up to the selected step.

# 2
# Extract and Load Processes

Tableau Prep Builder allows you to connect to a large variety of industry-leading data platforms.

When Tableau Prep was initially launched, the only outputs supported were flat files and Tableau native formats **TDE** and **Hyper**. However, since the *2020.2.3* release in August 2020, you can output to database platforms such as SQL Server as well, making Tableau Prep a much more appealing tool. It allows you to do the following:

- Ingest and output to flat files and a variety of database platforms
- Learn how to work with Tableau extracts

In this chapter, you will find recipes to ingest and output the data you require from and to a wide variety of data types:

- Connecting to text and Excel files
- Connecting to PDF files
- Connecting to SAS, SPSS, and R files
- Connecting to on-premises databases
- Connecting to cloud databases

- Connecting to Tableau extracts

- Connecting to JDBC or ODBC data sources

- Writing data to CSV and Hyper files

- Writing data to databases

- Setting up an incremental refresh

If you are connecting a BI tool such as Tableau Desktop to your data, selecting the appropriate output type may impact your Tableau workbook performance.

# Technical requirements

To follow along with the recipes in this chapter, you will require Tableau Prep Builder version 2020.2.3 or later. If you'd like to follow along and connect or write to a database, you must have the appropriate database set up and have an account with the appropriate access privileges.

The recipes in this chapter use sample data files, which you can download from the book's GitHub repository: `https://github.com/PacktPublishing/Tableau-Prep-Cookbook`.

# Connecting to text and Excel files

In this recipe, we'll connect to a **Comma-Separated Values** (**CSV**) file containing sales transactions and create a second connection to multiple **Excel** files. These connection types are very similar and so we'll cover them in one recipe. However, there are key features to both, which we'll highlight.

## Getting ready

To follow along with the recipe, download the `Sample Files 2.1` folder from this book's GitHub repository.

# How to do it...

To get started, ensure you have the sample CSV and/or Excel file(s) ready on your computer and open up Tableau Prep Builder:

1. From the Tableau Prep Builder home screen, click the **Connect to Data** button and subsequently select **Text file** from the **Connect** pane:

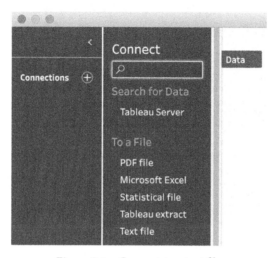

Figure 2.1 – Connect to a text file

2. Tableau Prep will bring up the file selection window next. From here, navigate to our sample file, December 2016 Sales.csv, and open it:

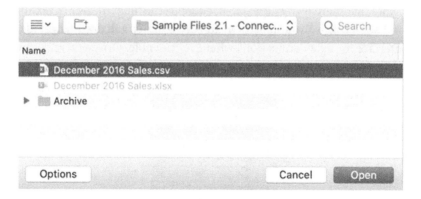

Figure 2.2 – Select December 2016 Sales.csv

Once selected, Tableau Prep will automatically create a new flow with the data connection in it:

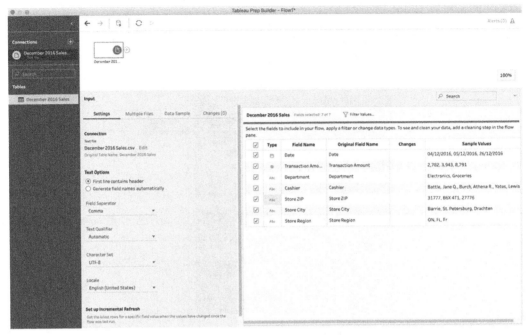

Figure 2.3 – A new flow is created when selecting any text file

Since the data connection is automatically selected, all options onscreen now relate to that particular connection. On the left-hand side, you can see the **Tables** pane. Note that there is only one table, equal to the filename. Since text files do not contain tables, this is by design. Tableau Prep Builder will always provide a generic user interface for data connections whenever possible. Once you're comfortable with one connection type, others should be easier to master:

Figure 2.4 – Text files such as CSV always have a single table

In the bottom pane, you can find a summary of all data fields identified in your text file, along with the automatically determined data type. In *Chapter 3, Cleaning Transformations*, we'll dive into the cleaning options you can perform here:

| | | | | | |
|---|---|---|---|---|---|
| **December 2016 Sales**  Fields selected: 7 of 7 | | | ▽ Filter Values... | | |

Select the fields to include in your flow, apply a filter or change data types. To see and clean your data, add a cleaning step in the flow pane.

| ☑ | Type | Field Name | Original Field Name | Changes | Sample Values |
|---|---|---|---|---|---|
| ☑ | 📅 | Date | Date | | 04/12/2016, 05/12/2016, 26/12/2016 |
| ☑ | # | Transaction Amo... | Transaction Amount | | 2,782, 3,943, 8,791 |
| ☑ | Abc | Department | Department | | Electronics, Groceries |
| ☑ | Abc | Cashier | Cashier | | Battle, Jane Q., Burch, Athena R., Yates, Lewis |
| ☑ | Abc | Store ZIP | Store ZIP | | 31777, B6X 4T1, 27776 |
| ☑ | Abc | Store City | Store City | | Barrie, St. Petersburg, Drachten |
| ☑ | Abc | Store Region | Store Region | | ON, FL, Fr |

Figure 2.5 – Field summary

3.   In the same bottom pane, you can configure the data connection settings. For text files, you'll always want to verify the **Text Options** section. Tableau Prep will automatically set these values as best as possible, but I recommend you verify them before you continue. The word **header** refers to the first row in your dataset. If you do not have headers in your dataset, you can select **Generate field names automatically**, which will create headers named F1, F2, F3, and so on. You can rename those fields later on. **Field Separator** tells Tableau how columns are defined in a CSV file, which is usually a comma or pipe symbol. **Text Qualifier** tells Tableau Prep which characters indicate the start and end of a value or string.

Finally, **Character Set** and **Locale** are typically identified appropriately but you can alter them here as needed:

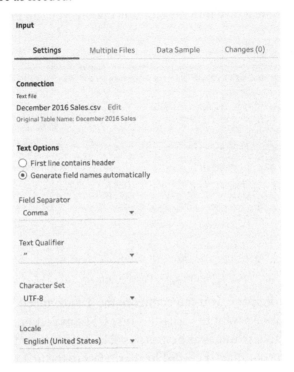

Figure 2.6 – Connection settings

4.  Now that we have connected a CSV file, let's create a second connection to an Excel file, in the same flow. To start, click the + icon in the **Connections** pane and select **Microsoft Excel**:

Figure 2.7 – Adding a second data connection

5.  Identical to the selection of a text file, browse to and select our sample file named `December 2016 Sales.xlsx`.

    Once we've selected the file, Tableau Prep Builder does *not* automatically show another data connection in the flow, as it did for our CSV file. This is the default behavior for any data connection that has multiple tables. In the case of Microsoft Excel, each Excel sheet is considered a table:

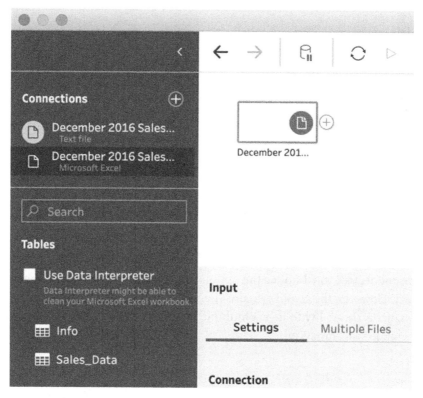

Figure 2.8 – Connections with tables require table selection before you can continue

6.  In order to continue, we must drag a table, or sheet, onto the flow canvas to finalize the data connection. Proceed by dragging in the **Sales_Data** table. Once added, you'll notice the color of this connection is different from the text file connection we made earlier. Tableau Prep Builder randomly assigns a color to the various data flows for easy recognition.

The colors do not denote any kind of functionality:

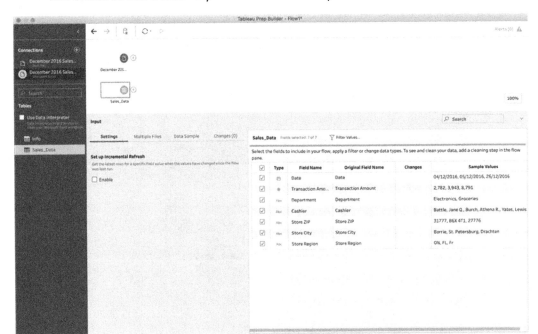

Figure 2.9 – A flow with multiple data connections

7. Once connected, you'll notice the options specific to text file connections no longer appear. However, the layout remains the same. A function common to both text and Excel files is the ability to ingest multiple files simultaneously. Select the **Multiple Files** tab for this function:

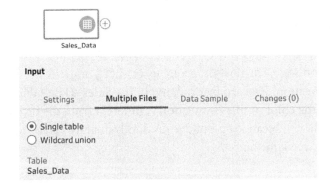

Figure 2.10 – Multiple Files tab

8. From here, select **Wildcard union** to reveal the options:

Sales_Data

**Input**

| Settings | **Multiple Files** | Data Sample | Changes (0) |

○ Single table
◉ Wildcard union

Search in
Sales Data                                                                    ▼

☐ Include subfolders

Files
Include                                                                        ▼

Matching Pattern (xxx*)
December 2016 Sales.xlsx

Sheets
Include                                                                        ▼

Matching Pattern (xxx*)
Blank = Include all

Included files (1)                          Include sheets (2)
December 2016 Sales.xlsx                    Info
December 2016 Sales.xlsx                    Sales_Data

Apply

Figure 2.11 – Multiple Files options

9.  Here, we can opt to include files in subfolders from the selected folder, which defaults to the folder where our Excel file is located. Select the **Include subfolders** option to enable this. Let's assume we want to include all sheets named `Sales_Data`, in all files ending in `2016 Sales.xlsx`. To do so, we can use the asterisk symbol as a wildcard and set the file **Matching Pattern** property to `*2016 Sales.xlx` and the sheet **Matching Pattern** property to `Sales_Data`:

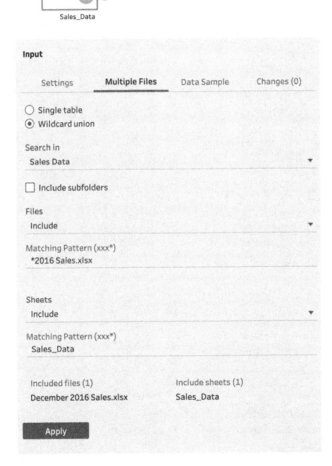

Figure 2.12 – Using wildcards to ingest multiple files at the same time

As a result, this step will now ingest all files in our subfolder named `Archive` and combine the data:

Figure 2.13 – All sample files here will be ingested at the same time using a single connection

By completing these steps, you have learned how to connect Tableau Prep to text and Excel files.

## How it works...

Tableau Prep text files and Microsoft Excel connections automatically detect most settings very well, so, in most cases, a couple of clicks will get you up and running. The most powerful feature is undoubtedly the ability to ingest multiple files at the same time. You can ingest hundreds of files at the same time using this method, using a single data connection.

# Connecting to PDF files

In this recipe, we'll connect to a **PDF** file containing text and a table with data. Tableau Prep has an exciting feature that can automatically detect the presence of tables in PDF files and extract the data for you.

## Getting ready

To follow along with the recipe, download the `Sample Files 2.2` folder from the book's GitHub repository.

# How to do it...

To get started, ensure you have the sample PDF file ready on your computer, and open Tableau Prep Builder:

1.  Tableau Prep Builder will not show us the entire PDF document, so it's best to open it in a PDF viewer and review what data we want to extract from our PDF. In our example document here, we have a single table and so we expect a table in Tableau Prep with the headers **Department** and **Amount**:

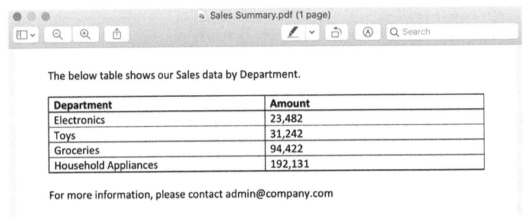

*Figure 2.14 – Sample PDF file with a table embedded in it*

2.  In Tableau Prep Builder, select the **Connect to Data** button, followed by **PDF file** to open the file browse dialog and select our sample PDF file, `Sales Summary.pdf`:

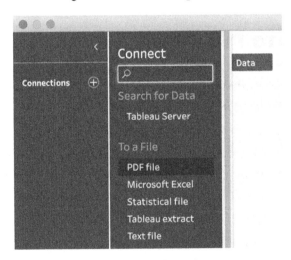

*Figure 2.15 – Select PDF file from the Connect pane*

3.  Once connected, Tableau Prep Builder will automatically detect the tables within the PDF file. In our sample, we can see the **Department** and **Amount** fields coming through as expected:

| | Type | Field Name | Original Field Name | Changes | Sample Values |
|---|---|---|---|---|---|
| ☑ | Abc | Department | Department | | Electronics, Toys, Groceries |
| ☑ | Abc | Amount | Amount | | 23,482, 31,242, 94,422 |

**Page 1 Table 1**    Fields selected: 2 of 2    ▽ Filter Values…

Select the fields to include in your flow, apply a filter or change data types. To see and clean your data, add a cleaning step in the flow pane.

Figure 2.16 – PDF tables are automatically extracted

4.  Each table is listed separately in the **Tables** part of the **Connections** pane to the left. This allows you to digest PDF files with multiple tables within them just as easily. The name of the table is automatically generated and refers to the page number in the PDF file and its position on the page:

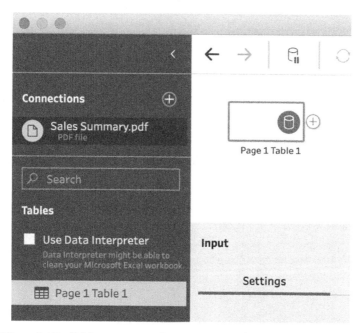

Figure 2.17 – Tableau Prep can detect multiple tables in a single PDF file

In this recipe, you have learned how to connect to PDF files and extract data for processing in Tableau Prep.

## How it works...

Tableau Prep converts each table in a PDF document into a data table when ingesting the file into a new flow. As such, Tableau Prep removes the complexity of parsing PDF documents and allows you to treat this like any other data connection.

# Connecting to SAS, SPSS, and R files

In this recipe, we'll connect to a **statistical file**. Tableau Prep offers fantastic integration with popular statistical files from **SAS** (**.sas7bdat**), **SPSS** (**.sav**), and **R** (**.rdata, .rda**).

I advocate the use of open file formats such as CSV or commonly used standards such as Excel. However, if you are unable to obtain your data in such a format from your data science partner, this connector may offer a solution.

## Getting ready

In this recipe, we'll connect to an R file using the statistical file connector. In order to follow along, download the `Sample Files 2.3` folder from the book's GitHub repository.

## How to do it...

To get started, ensure you have the sample RData file available on your computer. From the Tableau Prep home screen follow these steps:

1.  Click the **Connect to Data** button and select **Statistical file**.

2.  From the browse file window, locate and open our statistical file named `December 2016 Sales.Rdata`.

    And with just these few steps, Tableau Prep Builder has added the statistical file source to a new flow:

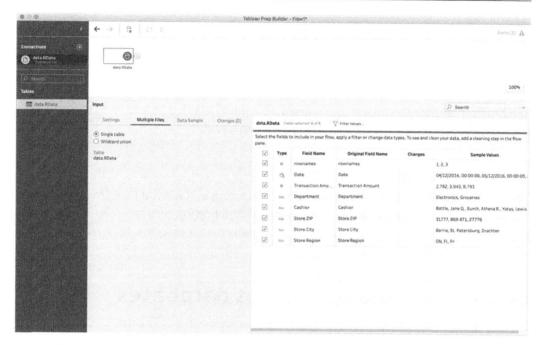

Figure 2.18 – Flow with a statistical file connection

Most options in the bottom pane are identical to those when processing Excel files. However, there is a small but important feature absent. You cannot alter the data type of the fields in the statistical file connection step. In order to do this, you have to use a **cleaning step**, which we'll discuss in *Chapter 3, Cleaning Transformations*:

| | | | | | |
|---|---|---|---|---|---|
| **data.RData** | Fields selected: 8 of 8 | | Filter Values... | | |

Select the fields to include in your flow, apply a filter or change data types. To see and clean your data, add a cleaning step in the flow pane.

| ☑ | Type | Field Name | Original Field Name | Changes | Sample Values |
|---|---|---|---|---|---|
| ☑ | # | rownames | rownames | | 1, 2, 3 |
| ☑ | 🗓 | Date | Date | | 04/12/2016, 00:00:00, 05/12/2016, 00:00:00, |
| ☑ | # | Transaction Amo... | Transaction Amount | | 2,782, 3,943, 8,791 |
| ☑ | Abc | Department | Department | | Electronics, Groceries |
| ☑ | Abc | Cashier | Cashier | | Battle, Jane Q., Burch, Athena R., Yates, Lewis |
| ☑ | Abc | Store ZIP | Store ZIP | | 31777, B6X 4T1, 27776 |
| ☑ | Abc | Store City | Store City | | Barrie, St. Petersburg, Drachten |
| ☑ | Abc | Store Region | Store Region | | ON, FL, Fr |

Figure 2.19 – Data types cannot be altered directly in the statistical file connection step

In this recipe, you have learned how to add Tableau Prep to a data science workflow by connecting to data produced by popular statistics applications.

## How it works...

Tableau Prep unpacks statistical files when you connect to them and, from that moment on, allows you to leverage them like any other connection.

## There's more...

There are some limitations when it comes to connecting to statistical files. If you run into any connection issues, I recommend you refer to the following section of the Tableau documentation online: `https://help.tableau.com/current/pro/desktop/en-us/examples_statfile.htm`.

# Connecting to on-premises databases

In this recipe, we'll connect to a **Microsoft SQL Server** database. The many connectors provided out of the box by Tableau Prep allow you to connect to databases almost as easily as to file connections, allowing you to quickly start an advanced flow.

## Getting ready

In order to follow along with this recipe, download the `Sample Files 2.4` folder from the book's GitHub repository. This folder contains the `Wide World Importers` sample database backup (`.BAK`) file, which you can restore to your SQL Server instance.

Note that the provided BAK file is suitable for SQL Server 2016 SP1 or later. If you're running an earlier version or need instructions on installation, please consult Microsoft's support page at `https://docs.microsoft.com/en-us/sql/samples/wide-world-importers-oltp-install-configure`.

## How to do it...

To get started, ensure you have Tableau Prep Builder open, then follow these steps:

1.  From the home screen, click the **Connect to Data** button to bring up the **Connect** pane. From here, select the search field and type in *SQL* to instantly filter the available connections.

2.  From the filtered selection of connections, select **Microsoft SQL Server**. This will bring up the **Connection** dialog.

3.  In this dialog, enter your connection details. Depending on your server, these details will vary. If you're not sure about these details, please contact your database administrator. Click **Sign In** to continue.

---

**Important note**

If you are using a macOS computer, the **Sign In** button may remain disabled even though you have populated the appropriate connection details. This could be the result of a driver missing on your device. To find the drivers needed, go to the Tableau **Driver Download** web page at `https://www.tableau.com/en-us/support/drivers?edition=pro&lang=en-us&platform=mac`.

---

4.  Once the connection has been established, Tableau Prep will show a dropdown in the **Connections** pane of all databases on the server you've selected. Select your database to reveal the available tables:

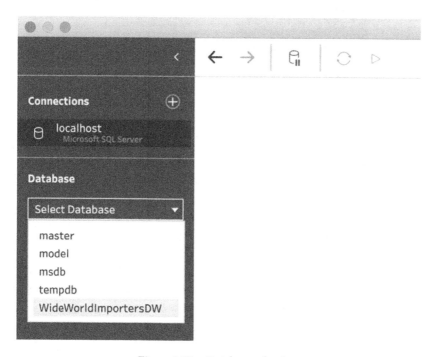

Figure 2.20 – Database selection

5. From the list of available tables, we need to select the table we'd like to ingest into our flow and drag it onto the canvas. Let's drag in the table named **Order**:

Figure 2.21 – Drag a table onto the canvas

With the table on the canvas, we can now continue building out this flow as with any other data connection type.

## How it works...

Tableau Prep has a number of built-in database connections that remove the complexity of connecting by configuring connections such as **ODBC** manually. The number of supported data connection types is continually expanding, too. If you do not see your database listed, you can always opt to use an ODBC connection instead. See the recipe titled *Connecting to JDBC or ODBC data sources* in this chapter for more information.

# There's more...

Database tables can relate to each other and be joined to each other to create insightful datasets. We'll cover joins in detail in *Chapter 5, Combining Data*. For now, I want to highlight a great feature in Tableau Prep that indicates the table **primary key** and **foreign keys** in the bottom pane. You can find this information in the **Linked Keys** section as shown in the following screenshot:

| | Type | Linked Keys ⓘ | Field Name | Original Field Name | Changes | Sample Values |
|---|---|---|---|---|---|---|
| ✓ | # | 🔑 | Order Key | Order Key | | 702, 894, 924 |
| ✓ | # | 🔑⊃ | City Key | City Key | | 50,969, 53,636, 41,165 |
| ✓ | # | 🔑⊃ | Customer Key | Customer Key | | 0 |
| ✓ | # | 🔑⊃ | Stock Item Key | Stock Item Key | | 163, 182, 197 |
| ✓ | 📅 | 🔑🔑⊃ | Order Date Key | Order Date Key | | 05/01/2013, 07/01/2013 |
| ✓ | 📅 | 🔑⊃ | Picked Date Key | Picked Date Key | | 05/01/2013, 07/01/2013 |
| ✓ | # | 🔑⊃ | Salesperson Key | Salesperson Key | | 11, 12, 23 |
| ✓ | # | 🔑⊃ | Picker Key | Picker Key | | 22, 17 |
| ✓ | # | | WWI Order ID | WWI Order ID | | 291, 357, 365 |
| ✓ | # | | WWI Backorder ID | WWI Backorder ID | | null |
| ✓ | Abc | | Description | Description | | IT joke mug - hardware: pa |
| ✓ | Abc | | Package | Package | | Each |
| ✓ | # | | Quantity | Quantity | | 3 |
| ✓ | # | | Unit Price | Unit Price | | 13 |
| ✓ | # | | Tax Rate | Tax Rate | | 15 |

Figure 2.22 – Linked Keys for database connections

There are three types of keys: primary, foreign, and keys representing both primary and foreign. Tableau Prep shows an icon indicating the key type accordingly:

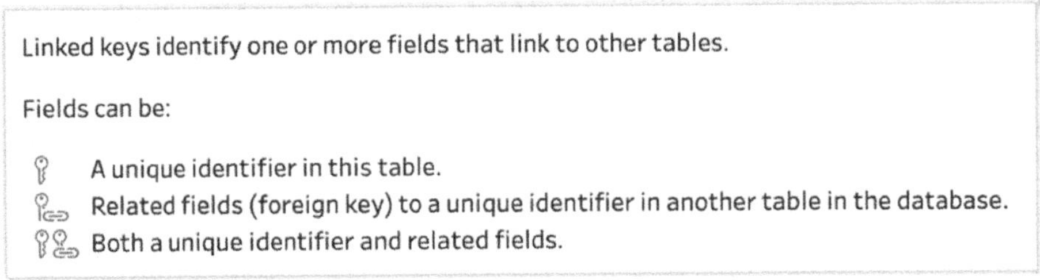

Linked keys identify one or more fields that link to other tables.

Fields can be:

- A unique identifier in this table.
- Related fields (foreign key) to a unique identifier in another table in the database.
- Both a unique identifier and related fields.

Figure 2.23 – Database key types

By completing the steps in this recipe, you have connected Tableau Prep to an on-premises database.

# Connecting to cloud databases

In this recipe, we'll connect to a local **Amazon AWS Athena** database. Just like on-premises data connections, Tableau has made it as easy as possible to connect securely to cloud data sources. You'll find many connections for popular cloud providers including **Microsoft**, **Google**, and **Amazon**. Each data connection dialog has been customized to the technology you're attempting to connect to. This means you won't see irrelevant fields for the selected connection type, reducing the complexity of cloud connections.

## Getting ready

In order to follow along with this recipe, you must have data stored and have access to that data in Amazon AWS Athena.

> **Tip**
> Getting set up on AWS Athena is beyond the scope of this book. However, if you wish to explore this option, the simplest way to get started is to create an account at `https://aws.amazon.com/`, then upload data to **S3**, and make it available to Athena by using **AWS Glue**. To use the same sample data as this recipe, download the `Sample files 2.5` folder from the book's GitHub repository.

## How to do it...

To get started, ensure you have Tableau Prep Builder open, then follow these steps:

1. From the home screen, click the **Connect to Data** button, then search for Athena in the **Connect** pane. Select **Amazon Athena** to continue.

2. In the **Connection** dialog, enter the details for your AWS Athena instance and click **Sign In** to continue:

   a) The **Server** field for Athena needs to be populated with the region information. The format for this is `athena.[region].amazonaws.com`. For example, `athena.us-east-1.amazonaws.com` or `athena.eu-west-1.amazonaws.com`.

   b) The staging directory is where your Athena results are stored in AWS S3 and follows the format `s3://[s3 bucket]/[s3 folder]`. For example, `s3://company/orders`.

   c) Finally, you'll need your AWS access key information. For information on how to obtain this, see the AWS documentation at `https://docs.aws.amazon.com/general/latest/gr/aws-sec-cred-types.html#access-keys-and-secret-access-keys`.

   d) You'll also need to install the Amazon Athena JDBC driver, which Tableau provides on its download page at `https://www.tableau.com/support/drivers`.

3. Next, select the appropriate **Catalogue** from the dropdown. In Athena terminology, this is the **data source**:

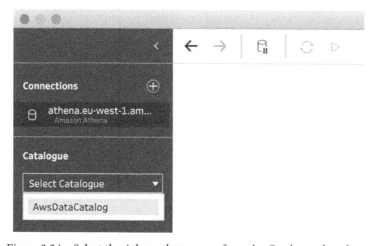

Figure 2.24 – Select the Athena data source from the Catalogue dropdown

4.  In the last step, select the database of your choice and drag the table you need onto the flow canvas. In our example, I've selected a database named **opssalesdb** and dragged a table named **results** onto the flow canvas:

Figure 2.25 – Selecting an Athena table

By following the steps in this recipe, you are now able to connect Tableau Prep to cloud databases.

## How it works...

Similar to on-premises data connections, Tableau Prep provides a simplified user interface on top of the database driver, so you can easily configure the connection. In this recipe, we've used the **Athena JDBC driver** in the background and configuring it is as easy as any other connections.

# There's more...

The following screenshot shows the clear mapping between the Athena web interface and the Tableau Prep UI:

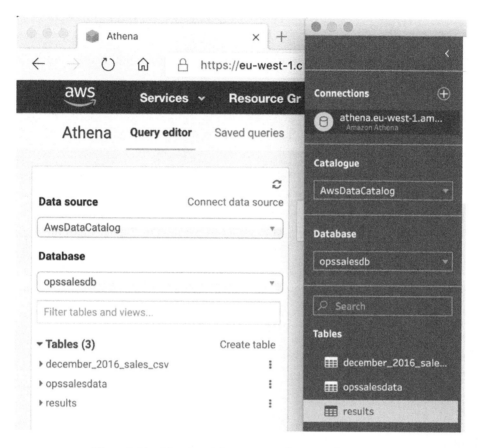

Figure 2.26 – Mapping Athena terminology to Tableau Prep

Let's move on to the next recipe!

# Connecting to Tableau extracts

Tableau has two popular proprietary data types, **Tableau Data Extract (.tde)** and **Tableau Hyper Extract (.hyper)**. Neither format can easily be read, if at all, by most data pipeline and ETL tools. With Tableau Prep Builder, however, you can easily use a Tableau data extract as an input into your flow. In this recipe, we'll connect to a hyper extract. The steps are identical when connecting to a TDE extract.

# Getting ready

To follow along with this recipe, download `Sample Folder 2.6` from the book's GitHub repository.

# How to do it...

To get started, ensure you have Tableau Prep Builder open, then follow these steps:

1. From the home screen, click the **Connect to Data** button. From the **Connect** pane, select **Tableau extract**. This connection type is suited to both TDE and hyper extracts.

2. From the file browse dialog, select and open our Hyper file named `Superstore Sales.hyper`.

3. When the hyper extract has a single table, Tableau Prep will automatically add that table to our flow. If the extract has multiple tables, all we need to do is drag the desired table onto our flow canvas to complete the connection. In this example, the extract contains a single table and is added to the flow by Tableau, completing our input configuration:

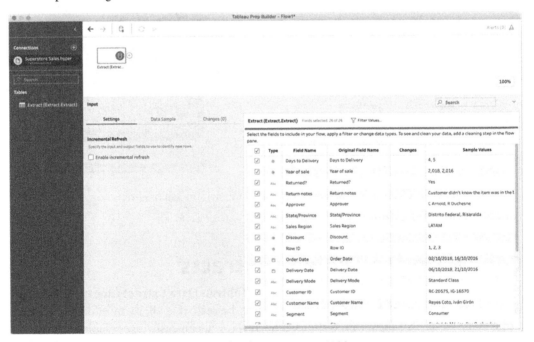

Figure 2.27 – Completed connection to Tableau extract

By following the steps in this recipe, you have learned how to connect to a Tableau extract.

## How it works...

As you've seen in this recipe, connecting to Tableau extracts is very straightforward, as you might expect from the company's own data source type. If you're fully into the Tableau ecosystem and using products such as Prep, Desktop, and Server, extracts are a great way to manage data and performance.

# Connecting to JDBC or ODBC data sources

Although Tableau Prep provides out-of-the-box connections to many popular data sources, there's always a chance you might be using another data source type. If this is the case, you can use **JDBC** and **ODBC** connections instead.

In order to use such connections, you must first install the requisite driver on the machine running Tableau Prep Builder and configure the connection outside of Tableau Prep. If you intend to publish your flow to Tableau Server, you must also create the same connection on the server itself, using the same **DSN**.

> **Important note**
> Tableau considers JDBC and ODBC unsupported connections and the success results may vary.

In this recipe, we'll walk through using an ODBC connection. The high-level steps for JDBC are largely the same.

## Getting ready

In order to follow along with this recipe, you must have installed the appropriate driver for the connection type of your choice and configured the ODBC connection in your operating system.

## How to do it...

To get started, ensure you have Tableau Prep Builder open, then follow these steps:

1.  From the home screen, click the **Connect to Data** button and scroll to the very bottom of the **Connect** pane to select **Other Databases (ODBC)**:

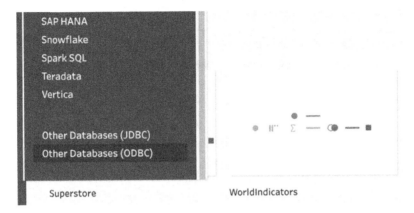

Figure 2.28 – Selecting the ODBC connection type

2.  The connection dialog for ODBC connections is very simple as the connection details are already captured in the DSN you have pre-configured on your system. All you need to do is select the DSN of your choice, and enter your credentials prior to selecting **Sign In**.

3.  Once connected, the options on the flow screen will depend on your data source type. In this example, our ODBC connects to Microsoft SQL Server and shows the expected selection options, including **Database**, **Schema**, and **Tables**. Once you've added your desired table to the flow, you can treat this ODBC as any other connection type.

> **Important note**
>
> For ease of demonstration purposes, this recipe shows how to connect to Microsoft SQL Server using ODBC. However, when available, you should always aim to use a supported connection type in Tableau Prep rather than JDBC or ODBC. This ensures optimal performance and reduces the chance of unforeseen errors.

## How it works...

Using JDBC and ODBC tells Tableau Prep to go to your system's respective data source connections, as referred to by the DSN name, and leverage the connection as configured. However, Tableau Prep cannot control these connections, its settings, or the drivers used. Therefore, they are not supported and should be used with caution.

# Writing data to CSV and Hyper files

In this recipe, we'll create an output to a file. There are two file outputs supported by Tableau Prep, Comma-Separated Values (`.csv`) files and Tableau extracts (`.hyper`). When you're planning to perform downstream analysis with Tableau Desktop, I recommend using Tableau extracts as they have great performance benefits. If, however, you're utilizing it for any other purposes, CSV is a great open format to utilize.

## Getting ready

Follow along with the steps in this recipe by downloading the `Sample Files 2.8` folder from the book's GitHub repository.

## How to do it...

To follow along with the recipe, open up a new flow in Tableau Prep Builder and configure a data input connection, using the `Superstore Sales.hyper` sample file.

Then, follow along with these steps:

1.  Hover your mouse over the data input step in your flow and click the + icon. The context menu allows you to select a step to be added to your flow in order to build your pipeline. In this recipe, we're focusing solely on the output, so select the **Output** option:

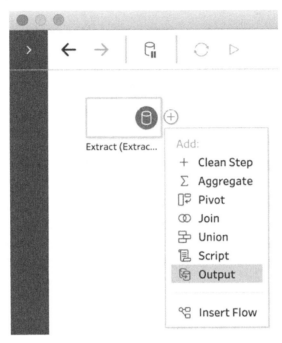

Figure 2.29 – Adding an Output step to your flow

2.  Tableau Prep will instantly add the **Output** step and select it, which brings up the bottom pane where the output configuration is visible, as well as a data preview.

3.  In the output settings, the default configuration is always **File** and the type is **Tableau Data Extract (.hyper)**. We can change the output **Name**, which is the filename, **Location**, and **Output type** properties here. The only other available type is **Comma-Separated Values (.csv)**. Let's change the location to the same folder as our input file:

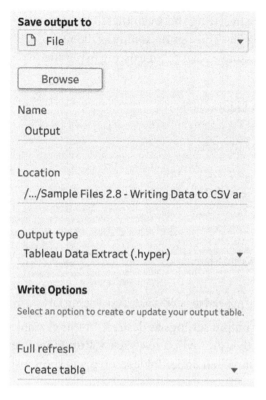

Figure 2.30 – File output settings

---

**Important note**

Saving to Tableau Server: If you'd like to save a hyper extract output to Tableau Server, you can change the owutput from **File** to **Published Data Source**. This will then write the **hyper file** to **Tableau Server**. This is *only* possible for hyper files and not for CSV files.

4.    The only difference in settings between these two output types is the ability to **append** an existing file. This option is only available for Tableau data extracts and will write the data as new rows to an existing hyper file:

Figure 2.31 – Append to table is only available for Tableau hyper extracts

5.    We can adjust our output settings as desired. In this example, let's leave all the default settings as they are. When ready, click **Run Flow** to execute your flow and generate the output. When done, Tableau Prep will show a success message.

6.    Let's browse our filesystem and verify that the output has been produced:

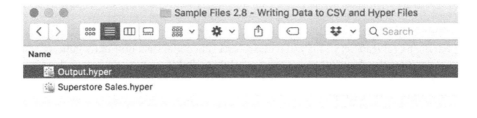

Figure 2.32 – The output generated by Tableau Prep

7.  Anytime you've created a hyper extract, you can easily validate the extract by connecting to it in Tableau Desktop, using it as a data source:

Figure 2.33 – Using Tableau Prep hyper output as a data source in Tableau Desktop

Using the steps in this recipe, you have learned how to write data from Tableau Prep to CSV and hyper files.

## How it works...

Using the **Output** tool, you can easily write data to CSV and hyper files for use in other analytics applications. If you save your output to Tableau Server, this is a great way to maintain those outputs.

# Writing data to databases

When Tableau Prep was launched, it was only able to output data to files, including hyper extracts. Thankfully, Tableau introduced functionality to write to external databases in release *2020.3*. With it, you can write the output of your flow directly to a database.

At the time of writing, the supported output types are **SQL Server**, **Oracle**, **PostgreSQL**, **MySQL**, **Teradata**, **Snowflake**, and **Amazon Redshift**.

# Getting ready

In this recipe, we'll write data to SQL Server. You can write to any of the supported types listed previously. Ensure that you have the appropriate database details and write privileges before you continue.

# How to do it...

To get started, open up Tableau Prep Builder and open the **Superstore** sample flow from the home screen, then follow these steps:

1. The **Superstore** flow has two output steps. Delete the second output by right-clicking the step and selecting **Remove**:

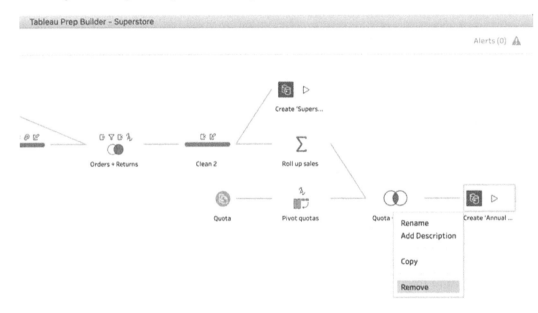

Figure 2.34 – Removing a step from a flow

2. Select the remaining output step, **Create 'Superstore Sales.hyper'**, to bring up the bottom pane with the configuration options:

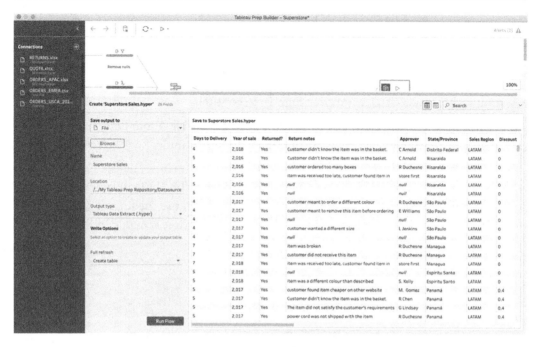

Figure 2.35 – Output configuration options

3.  Change the default output type from **File** to **Database table**:

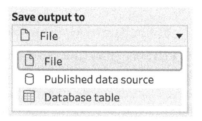

Figure 2.36 – Changing the output type

Doing so will raise an error. This is expected, as the new output location has no default configuration and therefore the flow wouldn't work if we were to run it now. As we configure the connection, the error will disappear:

Figure 2.37 – Incomplete output configurations cause an error

4.  From the **Select a Server** dropdown, select your server type. For this recipe, let's select **Microsoft SQL Server**.

5.  When you've selected a database type, you'll be presented with the same **Connection** dialog as this type would show for an input step. Populate the dialog with your server details and click **Sign In** to continue.

6.  Once signed in, the **Database** dropdown becomes visible. From here, select the database to which you have write privileges. In my example, I will select **Test Database**, which I created for testing purposes.

7.  Next, you can select an existing table to write to from the **Table** dropdown or create a brand-new table. When creating a new table, you can use the format [schema] . [table] to ensure you create the table in the appropriate schema. In this example, I'll create a new table, **superstore.test**:

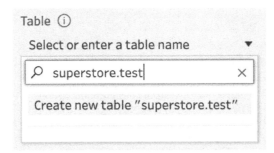

Figure 2.38 – Use [schema].[table] format to create a new table

8.  Finally, select the desired **Refresh** option. You can choose from **Create table**, **Append to table**, and **Replace data**. Make sure you carefully select the option appropriate to you, to prevent accidental deletion of database data. In this example, I'll select **Append to table**, which will create my **superstore.test** table in the process as it does not yet exist:

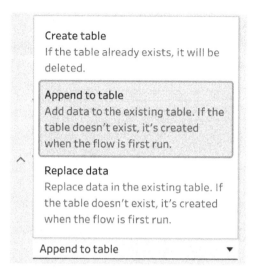

Figure 2.39 – Table refresh options

9.  When you're ready, click **Run Flow** to execute the flow and write the output to the database:

Figure 2.40 – Output successfully written to database

10. Using your favorite IDE, verify that the database table now exists, and that data has been written to it. I'm using Azure Data Studio with the query `SELECT TOP(100) * FROM [superstore.test]`. If all went well, your output will be successful:

Figure 2.41 – Verifying the output in the database

Using the steps in this recipe, you have learned how to write data from Tableau Prep to a database.

## How it works...

Using the **Output** tool, you can write data to a variety of database platforms. Doing so can add significant value to your use of Tableau Prep and allow you to prepare data for use with tools outside the Tableau ecosystem.

# Setting up an incremental refresh

Your flow may process a significant amount of data whenever it runs, taking up system resources, impacting database performance, and taking time to run. Much of your input data may be processed repeatedly as you run your flow. For example, your flow may process data from an order system. Running the flow daily might process *all* data just to capture the most recently placed orders.

In order to make your flow more efficient, reduce the burden on input databases, and minimize flow runtime, Tableau Prep allows you to set up an **incremental refresh**. In the example described, an incremental refresh would only process orders that have not previously been processed by Tableau Prep. To achieve this, Tableau Prep compares the data in the flow output to the flow input.

In this recipe, we'll configure a flow to achieve this.

## Getting ready

To follow along, open up Tableau Prep Builder and, from the home screen, select the **Superstore** sample flow.

## How to do it...

To get started, select the **orders (USCA)** input step, and then follow these steps:

1. From the bottom pane, select the **Settings** tab, then scroll to the bottom to reveal the **Incremental Refresh** setting and check the **Enable incremental refresh** box. This will result in an error message, which will disappear as we configure the incremental refresh in the next steps:

Figure 2.42 – Incremental Refresh settings

Tableau Prep needs to know three bits of information in the input step to configure a incremental refresh.

2.  Firstly, which field indicates whether or not a row in the data is new. In this example, we want to identify new **Superstore** rows by **Order Date**. Select this from the **Input field** dropdown to reveal the additional settings:

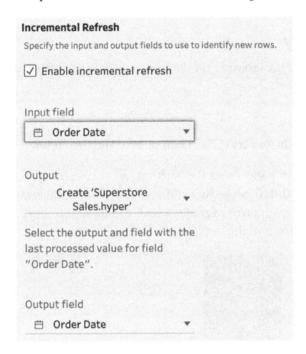

Figure 2.43 – Incremental Refresh field settings

Next, we need to tell Tableau Prep in which output it can find a field to compare the selected input field with, to determine whether a row is new or not. In this case, the fields are named identically, and so Tableau Prep has automatically selected **Order Date** as the output field in the **Superstore Sales** output, which is exactly what we want. No further changes are needed; your incremental refresh for this input is now configured. If you have multiple inputs, an incremental refresh must be configured for each input separately.

> **Important note**
>
> Replacing **Output** with **Incremental Data Only**: When you select the **Create 'Superstore Sales.hyper'**, output step notice the **Incremental Refresh** dropdown in the settings area. There are two options here. By default, Tableau Prep will append data, meaning only the newly processed rows are added. However, you can change this to **Create Table** to replace any existing output with new output containing only those newly processed rows.

## How it works...

Tableau has achieved a marvelously easy method to process data incrementally by comparing the existing output to the input for a particular field only. This method can save you hours of unnecessarily processing data that's already been processed previously.

# Publishing a flow to Tableau Server

Once you have created a flow, you may wish to publish it to Tableau Server or Tableau Online. When you publish a flow, you and others can execute it on-demand with a single click from the Tableau Server interface.

Furthermore, you can increase the transparency of your data flow for your report users, as they will be able to see a diagram of the data flow.

In this recipe, we'll modify a sample flow to output data as a Hyper Extract to Tableau Server, publish the flow to the server, and execute it from the web interface.

## Getting ready

To follow along with this recipe, you need access to a Tableau Server instance, either on-premises or with Tableau Online, with the appropriate privileges to publish data sources and flows.

> **Important note**
>
> If you're not sure whether you have the appropriate privileges, you will get an error message when attempting to publish your flow. Contact your Tableau administrator to request that your permissions be modified to allow you to publish data sources and Tableau Prep flows.

## How to do it...

Start by opening Tableau, then follow these steps:

1.  Before we get to work, we have to connect to Tableau Server. To do this, select **Sign In...** from the **Server** menu and then enter your server URL or select Tableau Online. In both cases, you'll be prompted to enter your server credentials. Enter your credentials and click **Sign In**:

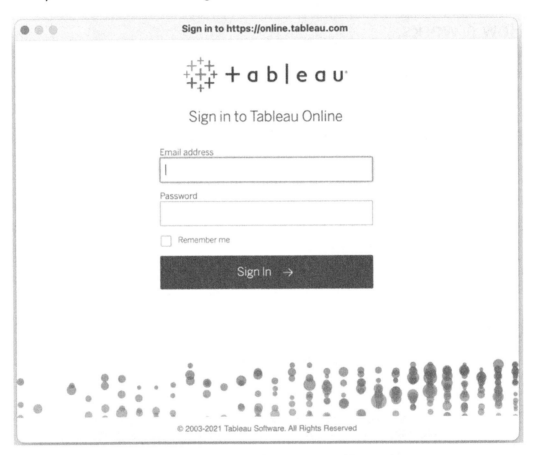

Figure 2.44 – Sign in to Tableau Server or Tableau Online

Note that Tableau Prep will not show any confirmation dialog to indicate a successful sign in. However, you can go back to the **Server** menu and, if you are signed in successfully, you will see the URL of your server in the menu instead of the **Sign In** option, as shown in the following screenshot:

Figure 2.45 – Sign in to Tableau Server or Tableau Online

2.  From the Tableau Prep welcome screen, open the **Superstore** flow from the **Sample Flows** section in the bottom left. This flow has two outputs, **Create 'Superstore Sales.hyper'** and **Create 'Annual Regional Performance.hyper'**, as shown in the following screenshot:

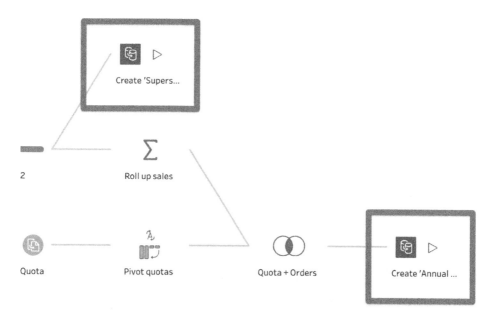

Figure 2.46 – Open up the Superstore Sample flow

3.   By default, these two outputs write a **Hyper** output to a location on your computer.
In this recipe, we'll change these outputs to write data to **Tableau Server** instead.
To do this, select each output step and change the **Save output to** setting to
**Published data source**, as shown in the following screenshot. Because we are
already signed in to Tableau Server, the **Server** address is populated instantly. We
can select a project from the **Project** dropdown. In this example, we'll use the
**default** project as our destination:

Figure 2.47 – Change both outputs to Published data source

4.  Next, let's save our flow to Tableau Server. From the **Server** menu, select **Publish Flow**. Set the project set to **default** and the flow name to **Superstore**. Click **Publish** when ready, to save your flow to the server:

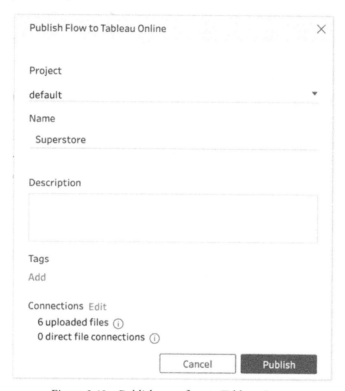

Figure 2.48 – Publish your flow to Tableau Server

5. When the publishing process completes, Tableau Prep will automatically launch your default browser and open up the flow. As shown in the following screenshot, a visual of the flow is present to help users understand the data flow at a glance. Click the ellipsis next to the flow name to open up the flow context menu. In the menu, select **Run Now**. When prompted with a confirmation dialog, select **Run Now** again to execute your flow:

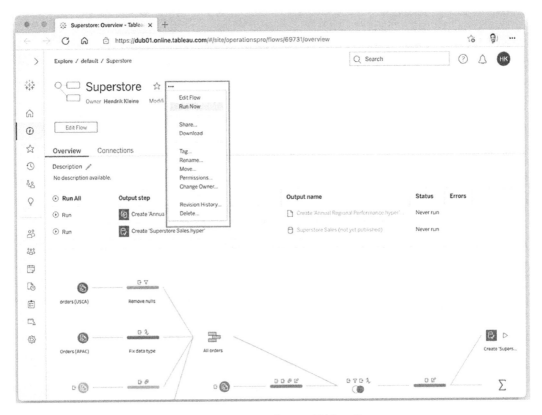

Figure 2.49 – Run your flow on Tableau Server

6. The Superstore sample flow does not consume many resources and depending on your server's configuration should take a couple of minutes to complete. Refresh the page to see the most recent status. When the flow has completed, each output will display a **Succeeded** status, as shown in the following screenshot:

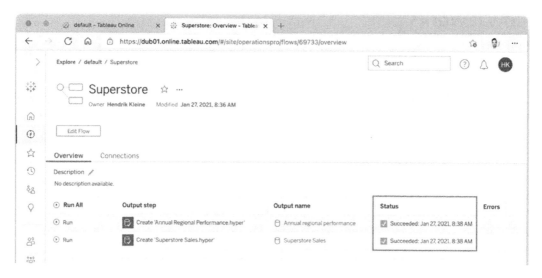

Figure 2.50 – View the status of your flow

7.  You can navigate to the **default** project folder by selecting **default** in the top-left corner. In the project folder, you'll now see the two outputs generated by our flow, **Annual regional performance** and **Superstore Sales**, as shown in the following screenshot:

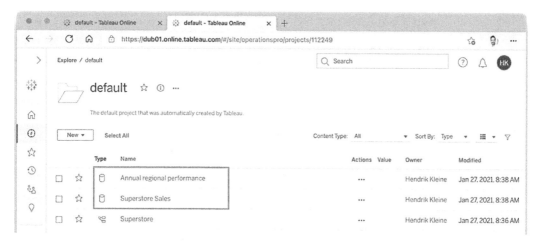

Figure 2.51 – Confirm the outputs have been created

With these steps completed, you've successfully completed this recipe.

## How it works...

In this recipe, we learned how to connect Tableau Prep Builder to your Tableau Server or Tableau Online instance. We published a flow and ran it on the server, with two outputs being written to the server. Publishing flows and data sources to your server is an excellent step toward offering transparency into the data lineage and transformation process to the users of your outputs and all subsequent reports created in Tableau.

# 3
# Cleaning Transformations

All of **Tableau Prep Builder**'s functionality is designed around the purpose of combining, shaping, and cleaning your data for downstream analysis. In this chapter, we'll look at the various transformations available to you to shape and clean your data.

In this chapter, you'll find the following recipes, which will help you transform your data:

- Renaming columns
- Filtering your dataset
- Changing data types
- Auto-validating data
- Validating data with a custom reference list
- Splitting fields with multiple values

# Technical requirements

To follow along with the recipes in this chapter, you will require Tableau Prep Builder. We'll use sample **Excel** files supplied in the book's **GitHub** repository, so there's no need to connect to a database. In each recipe, however, you can replace the suggested sample input data source with any connection type that suits your scenario.

The recipes in this chapter use sample data files that you can download from the book's GitHub repository: `https://github.com/PacktPublishing/Tableau-Prep-Cookbook`.

# Renaming columns

When it comes to cleaning data, one of the simplest yet most powerful actions might be simply renaming your fields to a more user-friendly format.

Tableau Prep steps can be categorized into three items: **inputs**, **transformations**, and **outputs**. During the first two, the input and transformation steps, we'll always have the ability to change any field name as desired.

## Getting ready

To follow along with this recipe, download the `Sample Files 3.1` folder from this book's GitHub repository.

## How to do it...

Open up Tableau Prep Builder and connect to the `December 2016 Sales.xlsx` file:

1.  Drag the **Sales_Data** sheet onto the flow canvas:

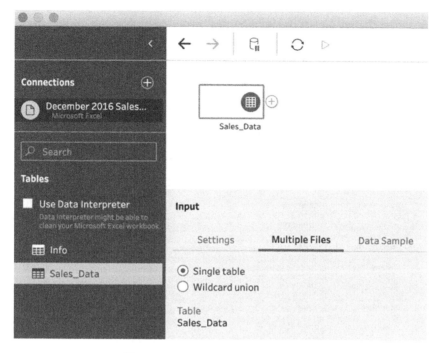

Figure 3.1 – Connecting to Sales_Data

When you select the **Sales_Data** input step, the bottom pane will show a preview of all the fields in the source data, along with their data type and some sample values:

| | Type | Field Name | Original Field Name | Changes | Sample Values |
|---|---|---|---|---|---|
| ☑ | 🗓 | DATE | DATE | | 04/12/2016, 05/12/2016, 26/12/2016 |
| ☑ | # | TRNSDATE | TRNSDATE | | 2,782, 3,943, 8,791 |
| ☑ | Abc | DEPT | DEPT | | Electronics, Groceries |
| ☑ | Abc | C_ID | C_ID | | Battle, Jane Q., Burch, Athena R., Yates, Lewis |
| ☑ | Abc | ZIP | ZIP | | 31777, B6X 4T1, 27776 |
| ☑ | Abc | STORE_CITY | STORE_CITY | | Barrie, St. Petersburg, Drachten |
| ☑ | Abc | STO_region | STO_region | | ON, FL, Fr |

**Sales_Data** Fields selected: 7 of 7        ▽ Filter Values...

Select the fields to include in your flow, apply a filter or change data types. To see and clean your data, add a cleaning step in the flow pane.

Figure 3.2 – These field names are not user-friendly

2.  In order to change any of the field names, we can simply double-click the current name, in the **Field Name** column, and edit it to our desired name. We'll always be able to see what the original field name was in our data source in the **Original Field Name** column. Go ahead and update the field names to match the following screenshot:

| | Type | Field Name | Original Field Name | Changes | Sample Values |
|---|---|---|---|---|---|
| ☑ | 📅 | Date | DATE | ☑ | 04/12/2016, 05/12/2016, 26/12/2016 |
| ☑ | # | Transaction Date | TRNSDATE | ☑ | 2,782, 3,943, 8,791 |
| ☑ | Abc | Department | DEPT | ☑ | Electronics, Groceries |
| ☑ | Abc | Cashier | C_ID | ☑ | Battle, Jane Q., Burch, Athena R., Yates, Lewis |
| ☑ | Abc | Postal Code | ZIP | ☑ | 31777, B6X 4T1, 27776 |
| ☑ | Abc | Store Zity | STORE_CITY | ☑ | Barrie, St. Petersburg, Drachten |
| ☑ | Abc | Store Region | STO_region | ☑ | ON, FL, Fr |

**Sales_Data**  Fields selected: 7 of 7     ▽ Filter Values...

Select the fields to include in your flow, apply a filter or change data types. To see and clean your data, add a cleaning step in the flow pane.

Figure 3.3 – Revised field names

It's easy to remember the changes we've made just now, but as your flow grows in complexity, it can become challenging to recall all the changes we've made. Tableau Prep supports us here by showing an edit icon next to the step in the flow that we've altered. In this case, this is the input **Sales_Data** step. We can hover our mouse over the edit icon to see a summary of the edits we made:

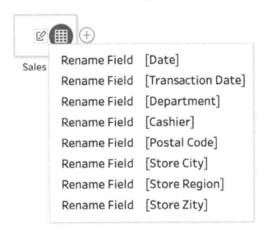

Figure 3.4 – Hover over any edit icon to see a summary of the changes made

Of course, you may wish to get more detailed insights into the exact change. There's a great overview of that as well! We can click the step with the changes and, from the bottom pane, select the **Changes** tab. This tab provides detailed insight into the changes made, and we can edit or remove any of the changes as needed from here:

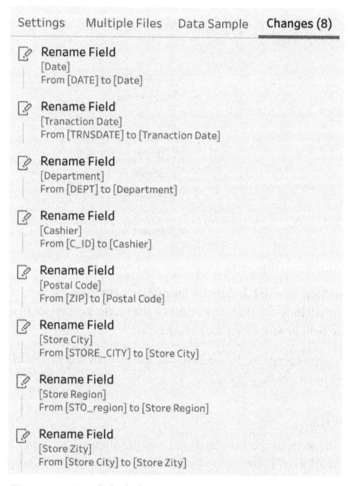

Figure 3.5 – Detailed edit history is available from the Changes tab

3.  You may have noticed a typo in *Figure 3.4*. We renamed the **STORE_CITY** field to **Store Zity**. We'll rename this to the right name using a slightly different way to the previous method, using a clean step. To add a clean step, select the + icon on the input tool and select **Clean Step**:

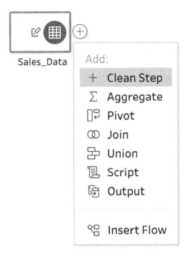

Figure 3.6 – Adding a step to your flow

4.  With **Clean Step** selected, locate the **Store Zity** field from the bottom pane, open the menu by clicking the three dots next to the name, and select **Rename Field**. Rename the field to **Store City** and press *Enter*.

You've now successfully prepared this dataset for use by providing user-friendly, descriptive names to all fields.

## How it works...

As we've seen in the steps in the *How to do it...* section, changing a field name in Tableau Prep is very easy. However, I recommend you take caution when renaming fields in your workflow at random steps. Doing so makes it more difficult for someone else to quickly understand your flow.

To avoid this confusion as best as possible, always rename fields as far upstream as possible, preferably in the input step itself. That way, your flow will stay organized and is easier to understand for others.

# Filtering your dataset

When preparing your data for analysis, it's good practice to provide the *least amount of data* required to perform that analysis. Our data inputs frequently contain data that is not required and that you may want to remove immediately during an input step.

Alternatively, you may transform your data in a Tableau Prep flow, and as a result, a field may become redundant at some point after the input step itself.

In Tableau Prep, there are three methods you can use to filter your data. In this recipe, we'll perform filter actions using all three methods: calculation filters, selected values filters, and regular filters.

## Getting ready

To follow along with this recipe, download the `Sample Files 3.2` folder from this book's GitHub repository.

## How to do it...

Open up Tableau Prep Builder and connect to the `Superstore Sales.hyper` extract file, then follow the steps:

1.  With an input step, the only method to filter our data is by using a **calculation filter**. To open up the calculation dialog window, click **Filter Values…** in the bottom pane:

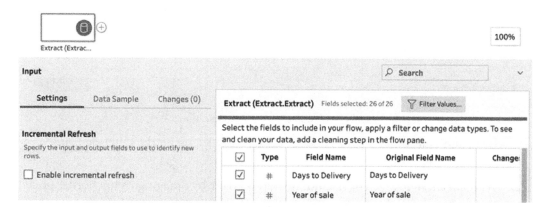

Figure 3.7 – Selecting the Filter Values… button to start a calculation filter

2.  The sample data contains information for three *segments*: **Consumer**, **Corporate**, and **Home Office**. Suppose we want to create a filter to only include **Consumer** information. To do so, enter the following calculation and click **Save** to apply the filter:

```
IF [Segment] = "Consumer" THEN TRUE ELSE FALSE END
```

> **Important note**
>
> Calculations are a powerful feature in Tableau Prep. You can find more information on calculations in *Chapter 7, Creating Powerful Calculations*.

As seen in the following screenshot, you can type in your code entirely, or use the reference section to look up functions and use the examples to get started:

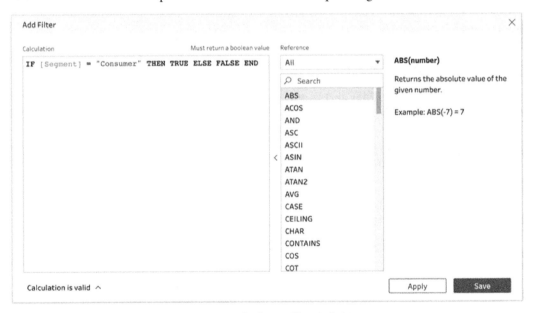

Figure 3.8 – Calculation filter definition

1.  Next, add a clean step to your flow by clicking the + icon on the input step and selecting **Clean Step**.

2.  With **Clean Step** selected, expand the bottom pane by dragging its top border up. Doing so will reveal a preview of your data. Depending on your monitor size and resolution, this pane may be visible already:

Figure 3.9 – Expanding the bottom pane on a clean step

3.  From the bottom pane, you can select any value in the profile pane, which will instantly update the data preview grid below it to show only rows with the selected value. Similarly, we can select multiple values by holding the *Ctrl* or *Command* key on the keyboard. Let's select **Office Supplies** from the **Category** field and **Binders** and **Envelopes** from the **Sub-Category** field. The data in the grid now only shows rows that have the selected values:

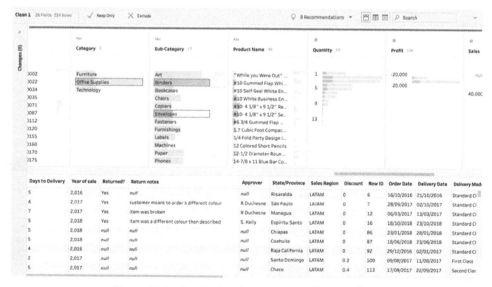

Figure 3.10 – Previewing data using profile pane filters

4.  We can turn this selection into a filter with a single click. At the top of the pane, you'll find that two buttons have appeared after we made our selection, **Keep Only** and **Exclude**. If we click **Keep Only**, Tableau Prep will create a filter to include rows with the selected values. Conversely, if we select **Exclude**, it will exclude those rows. Let's select **Exclude** to create the filter. You can see that the filter has been applied from the **Changes** section:

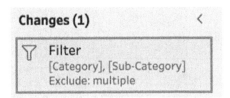

Figure 3.11 – Tableau creates a filter when selecting Keep Only or Exclude from the profile pane

5.  Behind the scenes, Tableau Prep has created a calculation filter for our last action. To see the filter, select **Edit Filter** from the **Changes** pane. Here, we can view or edit the calculation as needed:

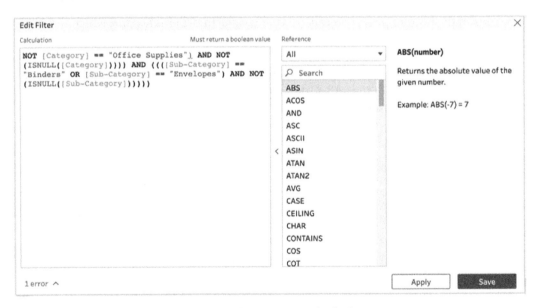

Figure 3.12 – Tableau-generated calculation

6.  Close the **Edit Filter** pane and add another clean step to your flow. In this step, locate the **Delivery Mode** field in the profile pane and click the more options menu, followed by **Filter** and **Selected Values**:

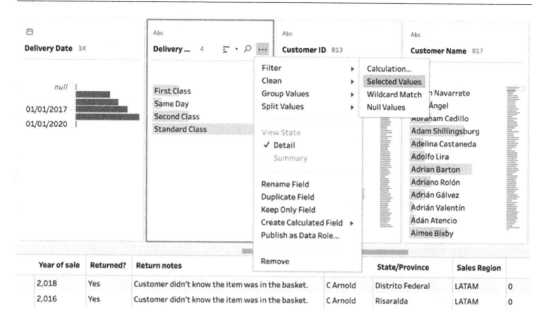

Figure 3.13 – Adding a filter from the menu

7.  The **Selected Values** dialog will allow you to choose from a list of distinct values in the selected field, to include or exclude. Let's select **First Class** and **Same Day** to filter the data to those values only and click **Done** to complete the filter setup:

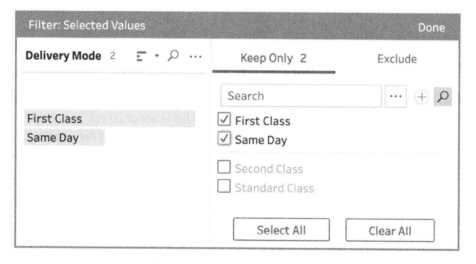

Figure 3.14 – Selected Values filter

8.  Next, locate the **Order Date** field and open up the filter menu once more. Notice how the options here are different than those we saw previously for **Delivery Mode**. That's because the options shown will always be relative to the data type of the field in question. In this case, **Order Date** is a *date* data type, and so we only see filter options applicable to dates:

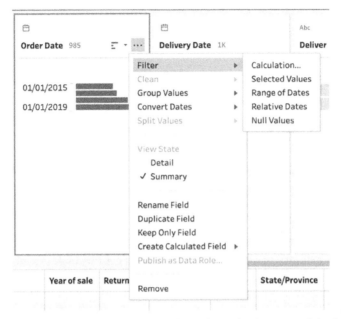

Figure 3.15 – The filter context menu depends on the data type of the field

9.  Select **Range of Dates** and set the filter to include data from *January 1st, 2016* through to *December 31st, 2016*. Click **Done** to complete the filter addition.

10. Next, open the filter menu for the **Product ID** field and select **Wildcard Match**. Suppose we only want to include values where the product ID starts with the characters FUR. To do this, enter FUR into the value match field and set the matching option to **Starts with**. This will exclude any rows that have a value in this field that does not start with FUR. Click **Done** to save the filter.

## How it works...

In this recipe, we learned how to leverage data filters in Tableau Prep. Filters are the primary method for cleaning your dataset to remove redundant data. Besides benefiting the output for analysis purposes, a leaner dataset can also speed up the execution time of your flow. For that reason, exclude unnecessary data as early as possible in your flow.

# Changing data types

With Tableau Prep's ability to connect to an incredible number of different data sources comes the challenge of *data type* management. Every data source technology handles data types slightly differently, or stores values differently. The wrong data type may limit the number of functions you can perform with that field. For example, you cannot aggregate a number if its data type is text, nor can you filter for a date range if the data type is not a date.

Tableau Prep does a phenomenal job of automatically detecting the appropriate data type. Tableau Prep data types are listed as follows:

- **Number (decimal)**
- **Number (whole)**
- **Date & Time**
- **Date**
- **String**

There are times when Tableau is unable to determine the correct data type, and times when it is unable to set it to your desired type because the values in the data are not compatible. We'll look at both cases in this recipe and how to address them.

## Getting ready

To follow along with this recipe, download the `Sample Files 3.3` folder from this book's **GitHub** repository.

# How to do it...

Open up Tableau Prep and connect to the December Sales 2016.xlsx file from the Sample Files 3.3 folder and follow the steps:

1. When you add an input step, Tableau Prep will show you a list of fields in the source, along with the data type it has automatically detected. The data type is indicated by an icon in the **Type** column. You can select any of the options here to change the data type instantly. In this particular dataset, we have two fields with a data type issue, **Date** and **Return Date**. **Date** has been detected as a number, whereas **Return Date** has been set to **String**. To correct this, click the icon type and set both fields to **Date**:

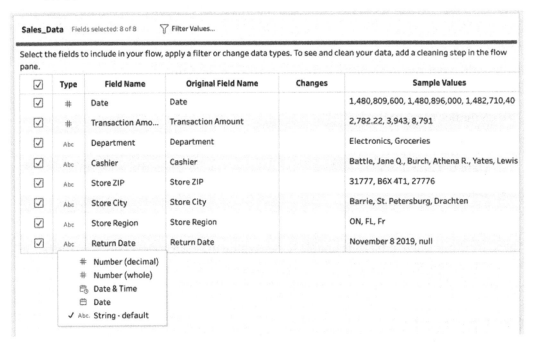

Figure 3.16 – Field list in the input step

2. Once set, you should see both fields list a single sample value of **null**. In this case, the input tool was not able to automatically change the data type to our preference. From the **Changes** pane, undo the changes:

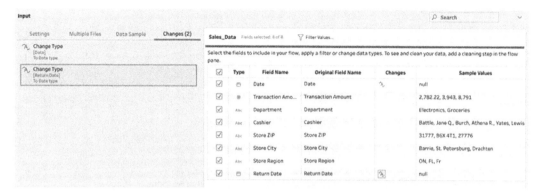

Figure 3.17 – null values appear after the data type change attempt

3. Let's add a cleaning step to the flow and from the profile pane, select the **Abc** data type icon above the **Return Date** field name and set it to **Date**:

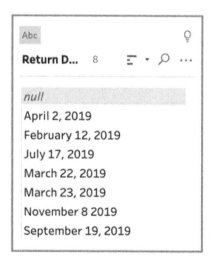

Figure 3.18 – Data types can be changed from the profile pane (Abc)

The change is successful this time and the pane shows proper date formats for the values now:

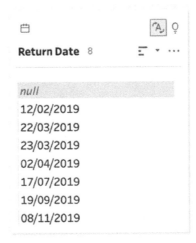

Figure 3.19 – The result of reformatting to Date

> **Tip**
> Always use the data cleaning tool to change data types. Not only does the result sometimes differ compared to using the input tool but you also have the added benefit of seeing more rows in the data grid, so you can instantly view the result of your changes.

4.   The **Date** column in our dataset is a little more problematic and cannot be solved by the cleaning tool itself. The values in this sample set are in *Unix timestamp* format, which Tableau Prep does not automatically recognize. We can however create a calculated field in order to return the date. To start a new calculation, click the **Create Calculated Field** button from the bottom pane. In the **Add Field** dialog, set **Field Name** to **Date Fix** and the calculation to `DATE(DATEADD('second', INT(str([Date])), DATE("1970-01-01")))`, and then click **Save**:

Figure 3.20 – Converting the Unix timestamp to a date

We can see that our new field, **Date Fix**, has been added and Tableau Prep has automatically set the data type to **Date**:

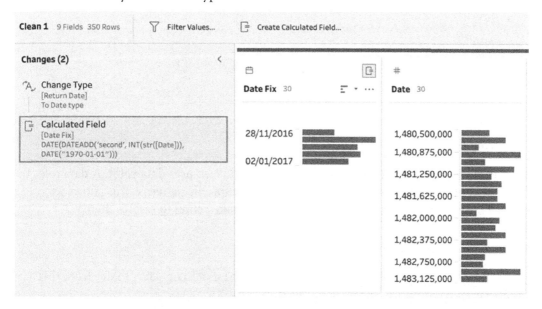

Figure 3.21 – A new calculated field has been added

> **Important note**
> Find out more about calculated fields in *Chapter 7, Creating Powerful Calculations*.

## How it works...

In this recipe, we learned how to improve the quality of our data by correcting data types. Tableau auto-detects a variety of data types for your inputs. As we've seen in this recipe, it also auto-detects the type for newly added fields that are the result of a calculation. If you ever run into issues with the automatic detections, your first port of call is simply selecting the desired type from the data type dropdown. However, advanced calculations are always available for more complex scenarios.

# Auto-validating data

Data validation can be a time-consuming task where we have to determine whether a value is accurate or not. One of the most typical data validation issues relates to misspelling and labeling the same thing differently. For example, the city of New York might be present in your data more than once, with different labels:

- New York
- NY
- NYC
- New York, NY
- New York, New York
- New York, US
- And so on…

To make the process of validating data easier, Tableau Prep uses **data roles**. A data role compares your data against a list of known values or specific patterns. This allows us to quickly identify problematic values in our data and take action to resolve them.

## Getting ready

To follow along with this recipe, download the `Sample Files 3.4` folder from this book's GitHub repository.

# How to do it...

Open up Tableau Prep and connect to the User List.csv file from the Sample Files 3.4 folder and follow the steps:

1.  To assign a data role to any field, we must utilize a clean step. Let's click the + icon on the input step and select **Clean Step**.

2.  In the bottom pane, from the profile section, we can see that our data contains three fields: Email, Profile URL, and City. We can use Tableau Prep's built-in data roles to validate the values of these fields. To enable validation, click the data type icon on the **Email** field and select **Email** under **Data Role** from the menu:

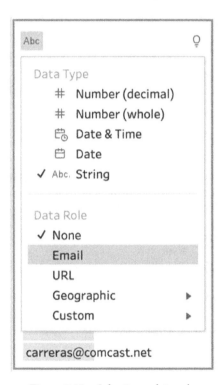

Figure 3.22 – Selecting a data role

With the role selected, Tableau Prep will validate the data in our sample file and flag any mismatch to the role with an exclamation symbol:

Figure 3.23 – Values flagged by a data role

We have several options to resolve these issues, which you can reveal by right-clicking an item. Let's select **Replace with Null** for `gator`:

Figure 3.24 – Edit options for data validation issues

Once you edit a value, you'll notice a little paperclip icon in the list of values and a change in the **Changes** section listed as **Group Values**. This is because Tableau has created a new group with the `null` value and added `gator` as a member of that group.

3.  Next, select the **URL** data role for the **Profile URL** field. Then, right-click the `Example` value and select **Exclude**. Notice how the value disappears from the list and the **Changes** pane now lists a filter to exclude this value:

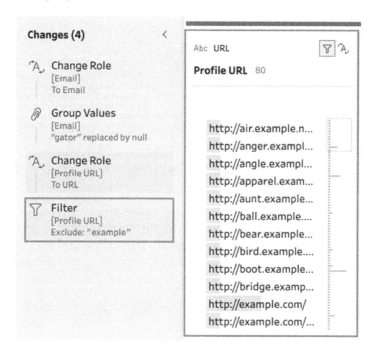

Figure 3.25 – Profile URL filter

4.  We can also create **groups** to resolve validation issues. Apply the **City** data role to the **City** field, then use the search function on the **City** field and search for **York**. This should result in two values, one of which has a leading space, resulting in a validation error:

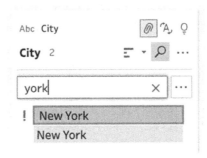

Figure 3.26 – Similar values

> **Important note**
>
> More details about the grouping functionality are provided in *Chapter 4, Data Aggregation*.

5.  We can safely assume that these values both mean **New York**. To group them together, select both (hold *Ctrl* or *Command*), right-click, and select **Group**:

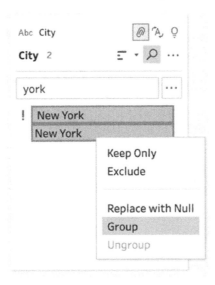

Figure 3.27 – Grouping distinct values

With the group created, we can now only see the **New York** value, and the warning has disappeared. Note that the **Changes** pane now displays another grouping action, specific to the **City** field:

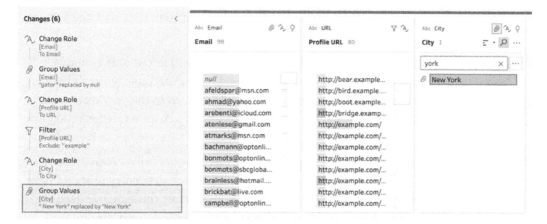

Figure 3.28 – Multiple grouping changes

You've now successfully applied auto-validation methods to your data.

## How it works...

In this recipe, we learned how to apply auto-validation to ensure the right information is present in our dataset. Tableau Prep relies on data roles to validate your data. The built-in rules allow quick validation of common fields. For more powerful custom validation data roles, refer to the next recipe in this chapter.

# Validating data with a custom reference list

Tableau Prep provides out-of-the-box data validation data roles for email addresses, URLs, and a variety of geographic fields. However, the real power of data roles comes from creating custom data roles specific to your environment and data. In this recipe, we'll create a custom data role and publish it to **Tableau Server** or **Tableau Online**. By leveraging your server, the custom data role can be made available to your colleagues, ensuring everyone is using a single reference list.

## Getting ready

To follow along with this recipe, download the `Sample Files 3.5` folder from this book's GitHub repository. In this recipe, we'll create a custom data role, for which you will need to be signed in to your instance of Tableau Server or Tableau Online.

# How to do it...

Open up Tableau Prep and connect to the `User List.csv` file from the `Sample Files 3.5` folder and follow the steps:

1. To assign a data role to any field, we must utilize a clean step. Let's click the + icon on the input step and select **Clean Step**.

   In the bottom pane, from the profile section, we can see that our data contains four fields: **Email**, **Profile URL**, **City**, and **Type**. We can use Tableau Prep's built-in data roles to validate values in the first three fields, as seen in the previous recipe, *Auto-validating data*. However, the `Type` field requires a custom role for validation purposes.

2. Let's focus our attention on the `Type` field. Let's assume we expect two distinct values in this field, `Consumer` and `Business`. However, data entry mistakes have resulted in other values being included. In order to validate this field, we need to create a custom data role first. To do this, open a *new* Tableau Prep window and connect to the `User Types.xlsx` file supplied in the sample data folder. This file contains the correct values for our `Type` column, against which we'll want to validate later. Add a cleaning step, then from the profile pane, open the options menu on the `Type` field and select **Publish as Data Role**:

Figure 3.29 – Creating a new data role

3. Tableau Prep will automatically create an output, which can publish this data role to your instance of Tableau Online or Tableau Server. It'll show a configuration error at first, which we can resolve by simply selecting the appropriate project to publish to. Select **default** as the project:

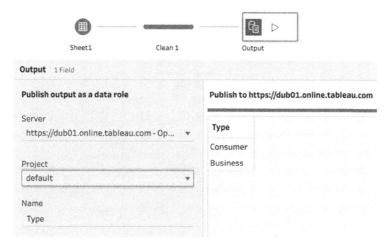

Figure 3.30 – Selecting the right Tableau Server/Online project

4. Run your flow in order to publish the role. When done, go to **Tableau Server** and confirm that your role has indeed been created:

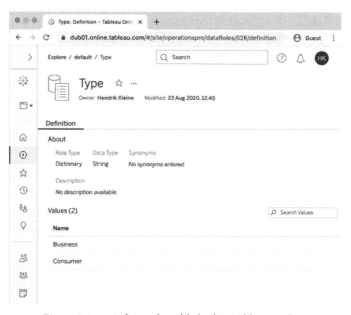

Figure 3.31 – A data role published to Tableau Online

5. Close this Tableau flow without saving and head back to our original flow. We'll need to reload it in order to get the latest data roles from the server. Save and close your flow, then open it back up and select the cleaning step. Now, select **Type** from the custom data roles section in the **Data Type** menu for the fourth column, **Type**:

Figure 3.32 – Applying a custom data role published to your server

6. Notice how Tableau Prep is now able to validate our data against the custom **Type** list from our server. We can quickly spot the mistakes and resolve them by using grouping to group the misspellings and to combine **corporate** with **business**:

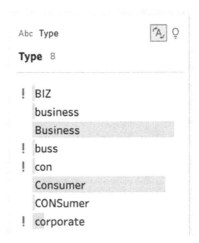

Figure 3.33 – Applying a custom data role published to your server

When done, your output should look as in the following screenshot:

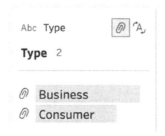

Figure 3.34 – Result of grouping

You've now completed the steps required to apply a custom data role using Tableau Server.

## How it works...

In this recipe, we learned how to combine the power of Tableau Server with Tableau Prep and create a reusable, custom data role. While built-in rules allow quick validation on common fields, the ability to create roles brings the power of reusable custom roles to your organization. You can create any number of custom roles and share access through Tableau Server so that you and your team can all leverage the same data roles.

# Splitting fields with multiple values

It's not uncommon for a single field to contain multiple values. For example, a name field may contain both a user's first and last name. Separating these can be done with Tableau Prep's **Split Values** function. **Split Values** facilitates the automatic creation of calculated fields with the necessary logic to split up a field based on your requirements.

## Getting ready

To follow along with this recipe, download the `Sample Files 3.6` folder from this book's GitHub repository.

## How to do it...

Open up Tableau Prep and connect to the December 2016 Sales.xlsx file from the Sample Files 3.6 folder and follow the steps:

1. Click the + icon on the input step and select **Clean Step** to add a cleaning step to your flow.

   In the profile pane, we can see that the field named **Cashier** contains an employee's name. We want to split that value into two separate fields, first name and last name:

Figure 3.35 – The Cashier field contains first and last names

2. Expand the more options menu on the **Cashier** field, and from the **Split Values** section, select **Automatic Split**:

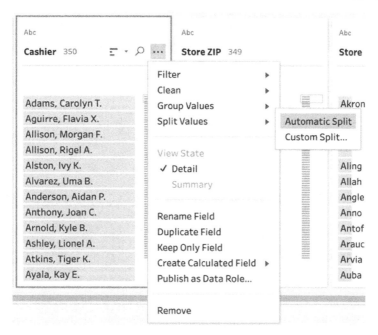

Figure 3.36 – Automatic Split

When selecting **Automatic Split**, Tableau Prep will attempt to identify the delimiter in the field automatically and subsequently create new fields as a result. If Tableau is unable to determine the delimiter, **Automatic Split** will display the **Custom Split** dialog instead.

The result of the action we just took can be seen in the **Changes** pane, where we can see that two new calculated fields have been created. We can also see two new fields in the profile pane: `Cashier - Split 1` and `Cashier - Split 2`.

Note that the splitting of a field does not amend or remove the original field. In this instance, we still have the original `Cashier` field present in our data:

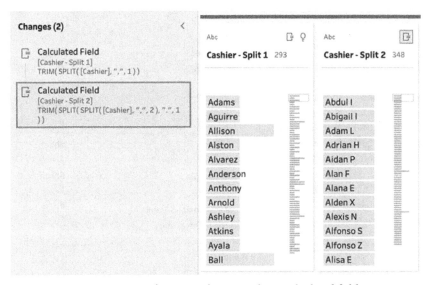

Figure 3.37 – A split action always results in calculated fields

3.  Change the field names of `Cashier - Split 1` to `Cashier First Name` and `Cashier - Split 2` to `Cashier Last Name`, then remove the original `Cashier` field:

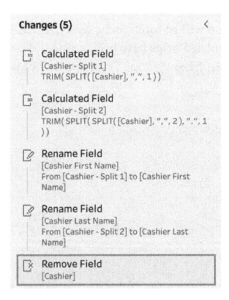

Figure 3.38 – Your Changes panes should look like this now

4.  We have another field in our dataset labeled `Store`. This field contains the store's city and region information split by a pipe, |, symbol. Let's split this field using the **Custom Split** functionality. Similar to *Step 2*, expand the options menu on the `Store` field, and from the **Split Values** section, select **Custom Split**. This will present the **Custom Split** dialog box, where we can specify the delimiter symbol and the number of fields we want to extract. Enter the pipe, |, symbol as the delimiter and split off the first two fields, one for **City** and one for **Region**. Then, click **Split**:

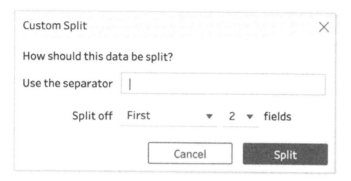

Figure 3.39 – Custom split

5.  Rename the fields from `Store - Split 1` to `City` and `Store - Split 2` to `Region`. Then, remove the `Store` field.

You've now successfully cleaned up this dataset and your **Changes** pane should look like the following:

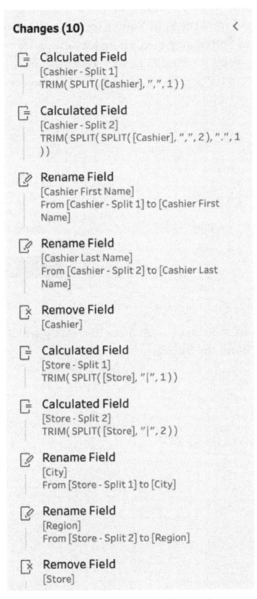

Figure 3.40 – A summary of all your changes

# How it works...

In this recipe, we learned how to split values contained in a single field into multiple fields. Whenever you create a split in Tableau Prep, whether you are using the **Automatic Split** or **Custom Split** option, Tableau Prep will create a **calculated field** to determine the values in the new field. You can always edit these calculations just like any other calculated field by selecting the **Edit** icon in the **Changes** pane.

The following screenshot shows the split function in the calculated fields dialog:

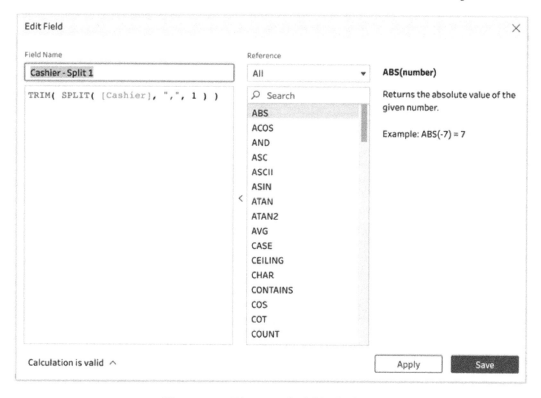

Figure 3.41 – Editing a split field calculation

With this knowledge, you can now manage complex datasets that store multiple values in a single field and transform them into an organized, easy-to-understand dataset.

# 4
# Data Aggregation

Tableau Prep is designed with data preparation for analytics in mind. When it comes to reporting and analytics, more data is not always better, especially if you have a particular report in mind that you want to create. Pre-aggregating your data in a data preparation tool such as Tableau Prep instead of your business intelligence tool may result in significant performance gains when it comes to rendering your report.

In this chapter, you'll find recipes to help you prepare your data for analytics. Aggregation is a key part of data preparation. Aggregating your data appropriately in a Tableau Prep workflow can significantly reduce the output size. A smaller dataset will be more performant when connecting any analytics application, including **Tableau Desktop**.

In this chapter, we'll cover the following recipes:

- Determining granularity
- Aggregating values
- Using fixed LOD calculations for grouping data
- Grouping data

# Technical requirements

To follow along with the recipes in this chapter, you will require **Tableau Prep Builder** and **Tableau Desktop**. We'll use the sample data supplied in the book's GitHub repository.

# Determining granularity

One key consideration that is often overlooked is determining the granularity of the data that's needed. For example, when working with geographic data, you may have values for continent, region, country, state, city, ZIP code, street, and so on. But if you're only going to report on country data, you may not need all those other dimensions. Or perhaps you are processing order data; you may want to consider whether you need the details for each individual line item in each individual order – maybe your analysis will be fine with just the total order amount per day. In this recipe, we'll look at a quick method to help reveal the data actually in use in a **Tableau Desktop** visualization.

## Getting ready

To follow along with this recipe, download the `Sample Files 4.1` folder from this book's GitHub repository.

## How to do it...

Start by opening the `Superstore.tflx` flow from the `Sample Files 4.1` folder in Tableau Prep, then follow these steps:

1. Click the **Create 'Superstore Sales.hyper'** output step in the flow and observe the number of fields shown in the profile pane at the bottom of the screen. These are all the fields that will be included in the hyper file when the flow runs:

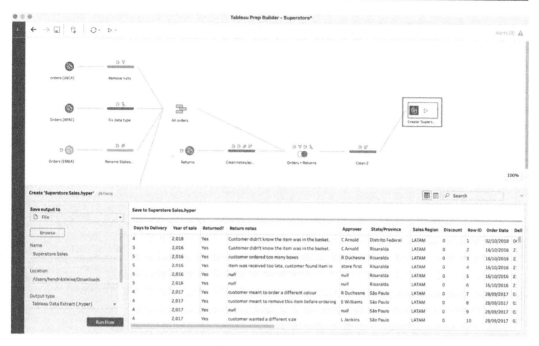

Figure 4.1 – Review the output fields in the last step of your flow

2. Click the play icon at the top of the screen to run your flow. If you've not altered the output settings, this will create the `Superstore Sales.hyper` file in your `My Tableau Prep Repository\Datasources` folder on your PC:

Figure 4.2 – Click the play icon to run your flow

3.  Leave Tableau Prep open and start up **Tableau Desktop**. In Tableau Desktop, connect to the `Superstore Sales.hyper` file you just created:

Figure 4.3 – Connecting Tableau Desktop to a hyper extract

4.  Click **Sheet 1** at the bottom of the screen to start a new visualization. To create the visualization from the list of available fields, drag **Segment** onto **Columns** and **Sales** onto **Rows**:

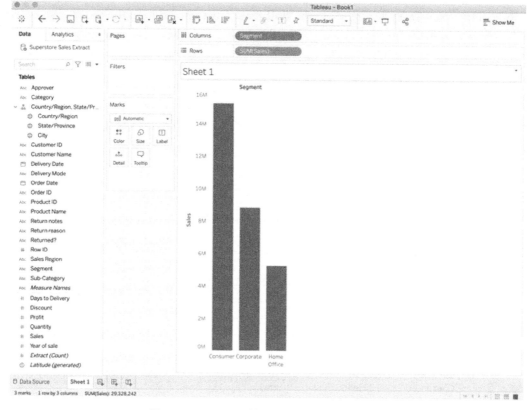

Figure 4.4 – New Tableau Desktop visualization

5.  From the menu bar, select **Analytics**, then **View Data**. Tableau will then display a dialog with the data that's present in the visualization. It should come as no surprise that the data contains the three segments and their sales amounts, as we saw in the bar chart. In the bottom right, you'll see that the row count is *3*. In a more complex visualization, you'll see all the data that was presented in this dialog:

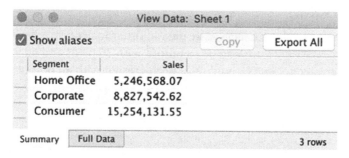

Figure 4.5 – Data that was visually presented in Figure 4.4

6.  In the **View Data** dialog, select the **Full Data** tab at the bottom, then uncheck the **Show all fields** option at the top. Finally, change the default preview value of **10,000 rows** in the top left to *50,000*. The value in the row box will automatically adjust the total number of rows, **40,889** in this case. The data that is displayed now is the data that Tableau Desktop processed in order to render the bar chart:

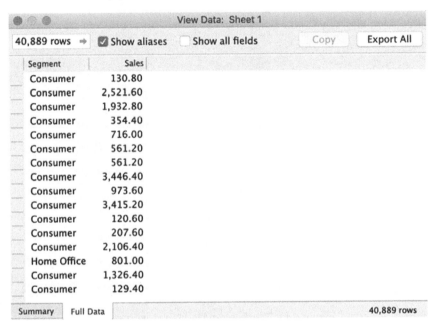

Figure 4.6 – Data that is processed in order to generate the visualization that was presented in Figure 4.4

In this example, we've determined that our data output from Tableau Prep contained many more fields than required to create the visualization. Furthermore, the fields that were required were more granular than required to render the visualization.

## How it works...

In this recipe, we learned how to aggregate data in order to achieve a desired output with the minimum necessary data. Instead of an output with 26 fields and 40,889 rows, the visualization we created in *Step 4* could have been created with an output of 2 fields and 3 rows.

What this demonstrates is that sometimes you may benefit from designing backward. First, determine the output, then determine what data and level of granularity is essential to produce that output. In this recipe, we've seen, using a very basic example, how we might want to start optimizing our flow output. As your reporting output becomes more complex, by adding more visuals, dashboards, filters, parameters, and so forth, designing backward becomes more challenging.

However, typically, the more complex and larger the dataset and output, the more benefits you may gain from choosing the right granularity and preparing your data accordingly in Tableau Prep.

In the following recipes in this chapter, we'll see methods for grouping and aggregating data in Tableau Prep.

# Aggregating values

There are several methods to pre-aggregate your data in your **Tableau Prep** pipeline. Ideally, your data will be aggregated in your data connection. For example, when connecting to a database, you may be able to write a query that includes a **GROUP BY** statement so that the data is aggregated before being ingested into Tableau Prep.

Often, such an ideal scenario is not available for a variety of reasons, and sometimes it is simply not possible, for example, when connecting to files such as **Excel** or **CSV** files.

In this recipe, we'll look at the preferred methods for most users when aggregating data in Tableau Prep, using the aptly named **Aggregate** step.

## Getting ready

To follow along with this recipe, download the `Sample Files 4.2` folder from this book's GitHub repository. In this flow, you'll find a slimmed-down version of the sample `Superstore` flow provided by Tableau.

The last step in this flow contains more than 20 fields and outputs more than 40,000 rows. However, let's assume we are interested only in the total `Sales` amount by `Segment`. In this recipe, we'll achieve that output using the Aggregate step.

# How to do it...

Start by opening the `Superstore.tflx` flow from the `Sample Files 4.2` folder in Tableau Prep, then follow these steps:

1.  At the end of the flow, click the **+** icon to open the context menu and select **Aggregate** to add the Aggregate step to your flow:

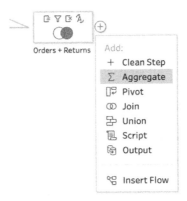

Figure 4.7 – Adding an Aggregate step

2.  Adding the Aggregate step will bring up its configuration pane at the bottom. Here we can select the fields that we want to aggregate by dragging them into the **Aggregated Fields** section. Drag the `Sales` field into the **Aggregated Fields** section. Notice how we instantly see the aggregated value of 29 million:

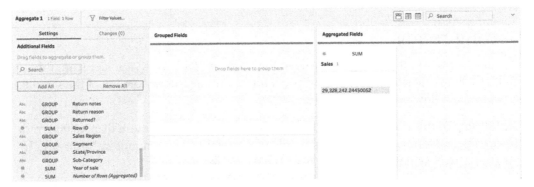

Figure 4.8 – Selecting aggregated fields

By default, aggregating a numeric value will be done by **summarizing** its value across all rows. However, you can select from a range of basic mathematic functions, as well as several statistical functions, to use for aggregation. To do so, click the **SUM** function on top of the field in the **Aggregated Fields** section, and select the desired function:

Figure 4.9 – Selecting a different aggregation function

3.   The preview we're seeing in *Figure 4.8* is our current dataset that will be output, and so we must add Segment back in if we wish to view the sales amount by segment. We do so by creating a group. You can create a group by dragging the desired fields into the **Grouped Fields** section. Try it out and drag Segment into the **Grouped Fields** section:

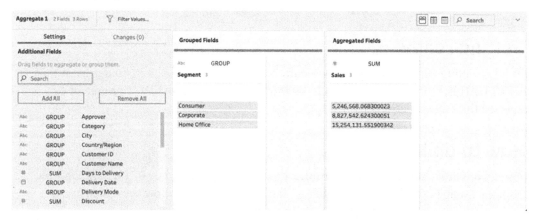

Figure 4.10 – greating Groups while aggregating

And with that, we've aggregated and grouped our data in just a few clicks. You can add other fields to the Aggregate step by simply dragging them into their respective sections. When doing so, you can always select a different aggregation function for each field. For example, you can summarize **Sales** but add the average **Discount** amount.

## How it works...

Aggregating data in Tableau Prep performs the calculations in the data preparation flow rather than outputting all data just for it to be aggregated later in a data visualization tool. It's a process that requires careful thought as you'll want to provide the optimal dataset for the intended downstream analysis: not too broad and not too narrow. In this recipe, you've successfully performed data aggregation. In the process of aggregation, you've created groups. Furthermore, the data preview in Tableau Prep itself might have given you the answer you needed without having to perform additional aggregation steps in a data analysis tool!

# Using fixed LOD calculations for grouping data

**Level of Detail** or **LOD** calculations are calculation expressions that have been available in **Tableau Desktop** for some time. An LOD calculation allows you to aggregate your data at different levels of granularity within a single dataset.

For example, you might have a dataset with customer orders, where each row represents a single line item in an order. You might want to aggregate revenue by order, or by customer, without losing the granularity of your data. This is where LOD calculations come into play. In this recipe, you'll create an LOD calculation. In doing so, you'll group your data into distinct buckets and aggregate values in a single step.

## Getting ready

To follow along with this recipe, download the `Sample Files 4.3` folder from this book's GitHub repository. You must have **Tableau Prep** version 2020.1 or greater to leverage the LOD functionality.

## How to do it...

Start by opening Tableau Prep and connect to the `December 2016 Sales.csv` file from the `Sample Files 4.3` folder in Tableau Prep, then follow these steps:

1.  Click the + icon on the input tool and add a clean step to your flow:

Figure 4.11 – Adding a clean step

2. Suppose we want to see the total **Transaction Amount** value for each department. As seen in the *Aggregating values* recipe earlier in this chapter, we can achieve that output with the **Aggregate** step. However, in doing so, we'd lose the LOD available. In order to prevent this, we'll create an **LOD** calculation. Expand the menu of the **Department** card, then, from the **Create Calculated Field** section, select **Fixed LOD**:

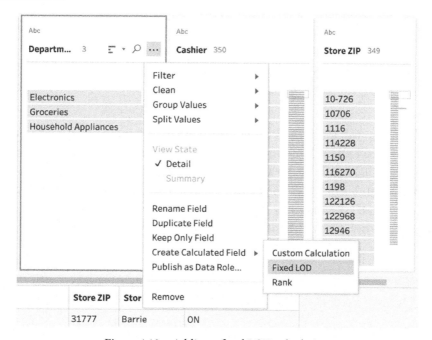

Figure 4.12 – Adding a fixed LOD calculation

This step will cause an immediate error in your flow. That's expected, as we need to take another step to configure the LOD calculation:

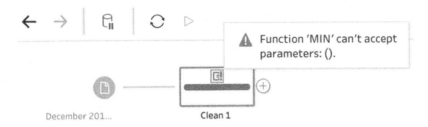

Figure 4.13 – Tableau Prep flow validation will raise an error with the previous step

3.  Now that we're presented with the **Fixed LOD** dialog, we need to populate the **Compute using** section in order to complete the calculation. In our case, we want to aggregate **Transaction Amount**. To do this, select **Transaction Amount** from the list of values and select **SUM** as the aggregation method, then click **Done**:

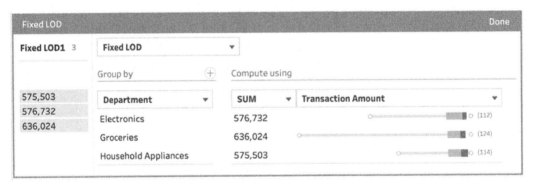

Figure 4.14 – Completed fixed LOD calculation

4.  Tableau Prep will instantly add a new field at the beginning of your dataset, named **Fixed LOD 1**. You can quickly rename this field to something friendlier by double-clicking the name and typing in **Total Transaction Amount by Department**. From the profile pane, we can quickly see the result of our action; the new fixed LOD field has only three values, one for each department. However, the original **Transaction Amount** field still exists with all its original values:

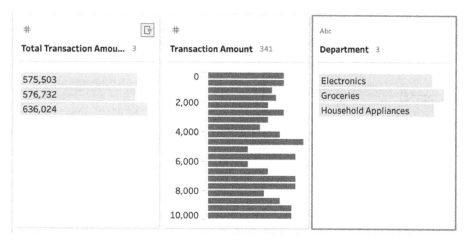

Figure 4.15 – Multiple LODs for Transaction Amount

> **Tip**
> Ensure that whoever is using your output understands the various levels of detail in your output. There are certain calculations that need to be avoided with the LOD field. For example, a graph plotting the `Department` and `Total Transaction Amount by Department` fields will have inflated results as it will summarize values that have already been aggregated.

## How it works...

Tableau Prep uses the same calculation expressions as Tableau Desktop. In this recipe, you've created an LOD calculation that resulted in the creation of a group and value aggregation in one powerful move.

In this recipe, Tableau Prep has done the hard work behind the scenes and created the appropriate LOD calculation based on our selections. You can view the calculation by opening the **Changes** pane:

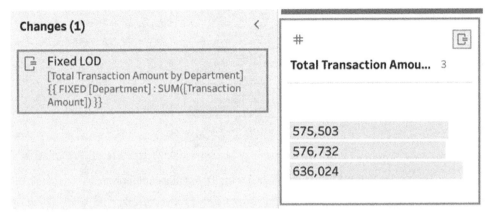

Figure 4.16 – Viewing the LOD calculation in the Changes pane

You're now able to leverage LOD calculations to perform quick data preparation, and even data analysis, in Tableau Prep!

## There's more...

To find out more about LOD calculations, you can download the **Tableau Desktop** whitepaper *Understanding Level of Detail (LOD) Expressions* from https://www.tableau.com/learn/whitepapers/understanding-lod-expressions.

## Grouping data

Grouping data in **Tableau Prep** can be done as part of the **Aggregate** step, as we've seen in the *Aggregating values* recipe earlier in this chapter. The function we'll review in this recipe is different, in that it can group values from a single field based on certain criteria.

As an example, values in a Name field might include John Smith and Smith, John. These might refer to the same person, and so we can group them together as John Smith. Performing this type of grouping is key to your data preparation efforts and ensures the downstream analysis does not run into issues with seemingly duplicate names.

# Getting ready

To follow along with this recipe, download the `Sample Files 4.4` folder from this book's GitHub repository.

# How to do it...

Start by opening Tableau Prep and connect to the `2016 Sales.csv` file from the `Sample Files 4.4` folder in Tableau Prep, then follow these steps:

1.  Add a clean step to your flow and observe the values in the `Department` field in the profile pane. We can see some of the data here has been entered inconsistently. Specifically, we have **Groceries** and **Grocery** and **Electronics**, **Electrics**, and **Electrics Dept**:

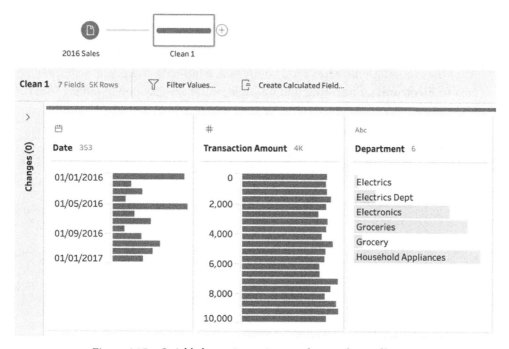

Figure 4.17 – Quickly locate inconsistent values in the profile pane

2.  Let's resolve the issue by using grouping. Select both the **Electrics** and **Electronics** (hold the *Ctrl* key on your keyboard) fields. Do not include the **Electrics Dept** value. Then, right-click and select **Group**:

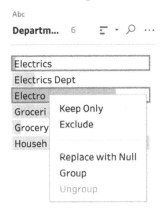

Figure 4.18 – Select Group in the context menu

3.  After the grouping action has been completed, a little paperclip icon will show up next to **Electronics**, indicating that multiple values are grouped together. Your data map changes over time and as a result, new values may be introduced. Let's assume the **Electrics Dept** value was added later. To edit the current group, right-click **Electronics** (the item with the paperclip) and select **Edit Group Members**:

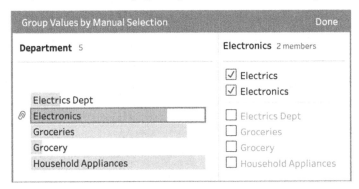

Figure 4.19 – Edit group members

4.  In the group members edit dialog, select **Electrics Dept** followed by **Done** to update your group to include all three variations of **Electronics**.

5.  Thus far, we've been grouping data manually, that is, selecting values and grouping them. Tableau Prep has a number of built-in algorithms that can perform grouping for you automatically. Let's try this out on the **Department** field by opening the context menu, selecting **Group Values**, and then selecting **Pronunciation**:

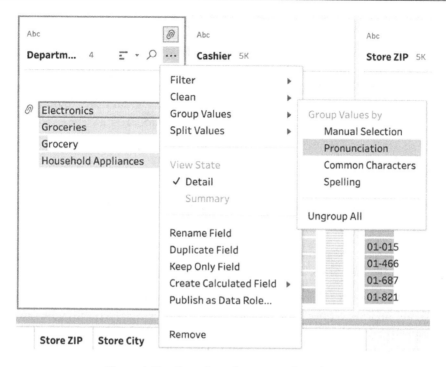

Figure 4.20 – Grouping values using algorithms

6.  The edit group member dialog opens up automatically so we can instantly view the results of this algorithm, and we can see here that it has grouped **Grocery** and **Groceries** together, as we wanted. Take note of how this edit group dialog is different from the manual grouping one we saw earlier. There's a slider at the top that influences the results of the algorithm. In this case, we see how similar the pronunciation should be in order to allow grouping. You can move it to the left and right to instantly see the effects it has:

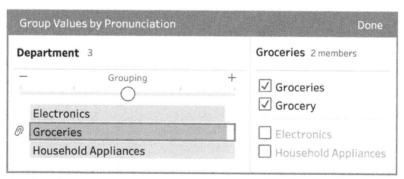

Figure 4.21 – Use the Grouping slider to influence the algorithm

## How it works...

In this recipe, you've manually grouped data. You've also reviewed the different options available to you, including manual grouping, pronunciation, common characters, and spelling grouping options. When you run your flow, Tableau Prep will replace any value in your group with the name of the group itself. Grouping is a great thing to do to improve the quality of your data and make the resulting analysis more robust.

## There's more...

There are three algorithms you can use for the automated grouping of values in Tableau Prep. Here is a summary of each of them. Each of these is available from the **Group** menu:

- **Pronunciation**: Using the `Metaphone 3` algorithm, this option groups words by their pronunciation. It's particularly useful for the English language.

- **Common characters**: This option looks at the `ngram fingerprint` of a value. In doing so, it determines the characters in common between different values, irrespective of order. For example, the names `Michael David` and `David, Michaels` have similar characters and will be grouped together.

- **Spelling**: Using the **Levenshtein distance** algorithm, Tableau Prep will group values with similar spelling. This is particularly useful when your data has text entries where you expect similar values, but misspellings may occur. Unlike the pronunciation option, the spelling option works for any language.

With the knowledge gained in this recipe, you're now able to leverage the different types of data grouping options available to you in Tableau Prep.

# 5
# Combining Data

Besides cleaning up your data inputs, Tableau Prep can be used to increase the value of your new dataset by augmenting it with complementary data. This can be done by extending the dataset vertically, adding more rows, or horizontally, by adding new data columns. Performing such data preparation tasks within Tableau Prep allows you to create a dataset that includes key data from multiple inputs, making the end result a comprehensive dataset for analysis.

In this chapter, you will learn how to combine different datasets by using a variety of different methods. Combining data is one of the most common actions in data preparation. Most organizations source data from multiple systems and combining that data into a holistic dataset allows more insightful analysis than looking at each dataset in isolation.

In this chapter, you'll find the following recipes to help you combine your data for analytics:

- Combining data with Union
- Combining data ingest and Union actions
- Combining datasets using an inner join
- Combining datasets using a left or right join
- Expanding datasets using a full outer join
- Expanding datasets using a not inner join

# Technical requirements

To follow along with the recipes in this chapter, you will require **Tableau Prep Builder**. The recipes in this chapter use sample data files that you can download from the book's GitHub repository at `https://github.com/PacktPublishing/Tableau-Prep-Cookbook`.

# Combining data with Union

Data is typically produced by multiple systems and certain systems may produce similar data that needs to be combined vertically. That is, the rows need to be stacked on top of one another. A use case we'll use in this recipe is combining sales data from two different sales systems, in order to get the total sales dataset prepared. This is a typical scenario you may encounter when your organization is operating multiple systems, is migrating from one system to another, is maintaining legacy systems, or is integrating systems from a partner or acquired company. In this recipe, we'll combine multiple datasets using Union.

## Getting ready

To follow along with this recipe, download the `Sample Files 5.1` folder from this book's GitHub repository.

## How to do it...

Start by opening **Tableau Prep** and perform the following steps:

1. Connect to the `DataExport_NOV_Sales.csv` text file in order to create a brand-new flow with a data connection. Let's assume that this is data from a legacy sale system, where each row represents a sale made.

2. Create a second data connection to the `DataExport_NOV_SalesData.csv` text file. This data is from the same legacy system, but it may reside on a separate server, resulting in the need for a separate connection here:

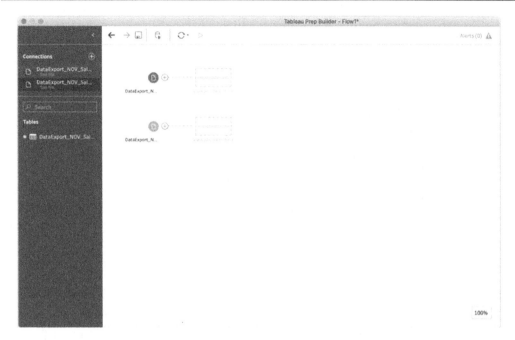

Figure 5.1 – Two connections to legacy system data

3.   We'll now need to combine data from both connections in order to get a complete picture of all sales made. To do so, we're going to union these two data inputs. To do so, click and hold the second data input and then drag it on top of the first data input. When you do so, you will see two options appear, **Union** and **Join**:

Figure 5.2 – Dragging one data connection on top of another for Union and Join options

Drag the connection so that **Union** is highlighted, and then release. Tableau Prep will instantly add a step named **Union 1**:

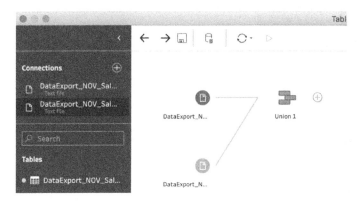

Figure 5.3 – A Union step is added by Tableau Prep when releasing the mouse

4.  Select the **Union 1** step to view the data pane at the bottom of the screen. Expand the bottom pane so that the data preview becomes visible. Notice how a new field has been added automatically, named **Table Names**. This field indicates the original source of each row in the combined dataset. You can scroll through the preview to see both values, **DataExport_NOV_Sales.csv** and **DataExport_NOV_SalesData.csv**:

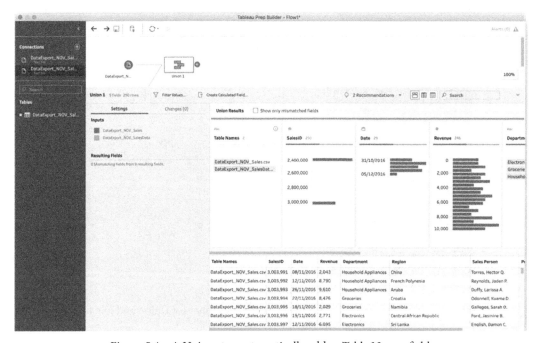

Figure 5.4 – A Union step automatically adds a Table Names field

> **Important note**
>
> In the bottom pane, take note of the two colors Tableau Prep has assigned to each data connection; blue for DataExport_NOV_Sales.csv and amber for DataExport_NOV_SalesData.csv. Observe the column headers and notice the multi-colored bar beneath all the field names, with the exception of the **Table Names** field. This multi-colored bar indicates from which data connection the field was sourced. In our case, all bars are a combination of blue and amber, meaning data was sourced from both data connections.

5.  Now let's add a third data connection to your flow. This time, connect to the POS_ Sales_Data_November_2016.xlsx file, specifically, the Sales_Data sheet. This data is from a completely different sales system. As a result, the data in the file is organized differently from the two connections we've used so far. Observe the input field names by selecting the input step:

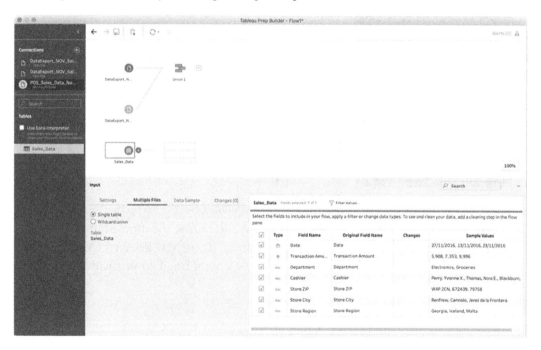

Figure 5.5 – Reviewing the input field name differences

6.  Even though we've observed different field names, we can still stack this data with the existing connections, using **Union**. Go ahead and drag and drop the POS_ Sales_Data_November_2016.xlsx input on top of the **Union 1** step. Notice how this time, three options appear when hovering, instead of the two options we saw in *Step 3* earlier. We have **Add**, **Union**, and **Join**:

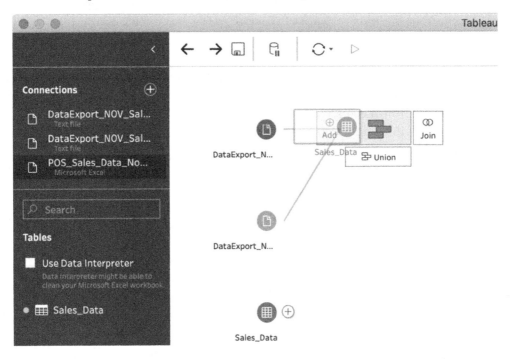

Figure 5.6 – Hovering over an existing union shows the Add action

Hover to the left to highlight the **Add** action and release the mouse button. This will add the third source to your existing union. If you have selected **Union** instead, a second union step would have been created, combining **Union 1** with the third data connection.

7.  Select the **Union 1** step to view the bottom pane. Notice how you can use the color coding to quickly find potential issues with the union. The **Inputs** section now defines three colors; blue for DataExport_NOV_Sales.csv, amber for DataExport_NOV_SalesData.csv, and red for our newly added POS_Sales_Data_November_2016.xlsx connection:

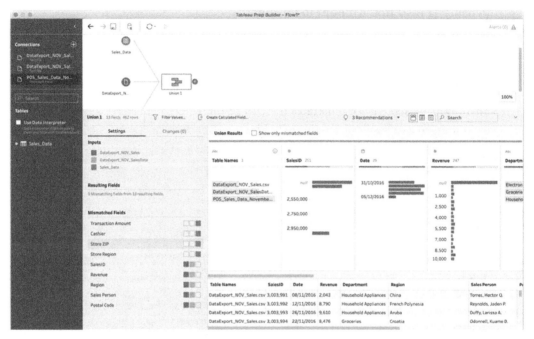

Figure 5.7 – Using color coding to quickly spot potential union issues

Using the same color bars we described in *Step 4*, you can quickly see the origins of each field. For example, **SalesID** is blue and amber, meaning it contains data from those two data connections. That is, the **SalesID** field does not exist in the POS_Sales_Data_November_2016.xlsx data connection. Similarly, the **Date** field has three colors – blue, amber, and red – indicating the field is present in all three inputs.

8.  The **Mismatched Fields** section uses color coding to inform us of the field origins, similar to the multi-colored bar under each field name. There are some fields that contain similar data, such as **Store Region** and **Region**. However, because the field names in the data connections are different, Tableau Prep was unable to align them in a single field. To solve this issue, we can simply rename the fields:

Rename **Transaction Amount** to **Revenue**.

Rename **Cashier** to **Sales Person**.

Rename **Store ZIP** to **Postal Code**.

Rename **Store Region** to **Region**.

The following screenshot illustrates the end result, where fields have automatically been merged as a result of renaming field names:

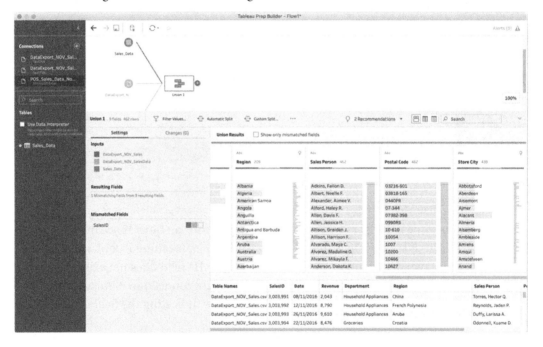

Figure 5.8 – Aligning fields by renaming them to a common name

As you can see, Tableau Prep automatically and instantly re-aligns the fields once they have identical names. In our case, we have one field remaining that is not present in the POS_Sales_Data_November_2016.xlsx data connection – **SalesID**. This is not an issue for the union step. The field will be retained, and any rows originating from the POS_Sales_Data_November_2016.xlsx data connection will have a null value for that field.

## How it works...

Tableau Prep stacks rows from any input to a union on top of each other and aligns the data by field names at the same time. In our recipe, we've resolved two scenarios. First, we combined data from two similar, but separate, data connections. In this case, Tableau Prep combined the data without any issues. Then we combined data that was significantly different, that is, data with a different number of fields, and different field names. Tableau resolves this by setting the value to null for fields that are not present in a certain input, and we can manually rename fields in order to trigger Tableau to align them.

# Combining data ingest and Union actions

When you have multiple data sources that need to be vertically stacked using a union, you may opt to perform that action during ingestion. This avoids you having to create a separate **Union** step in Tableau Prep. Furthermore, you can use wildcards in your input, such that the input becomes dynamic, and new data files can be ingested as they are added. A typical scenario for this would be an automated process that exports data on a recurring schedule, which you then need to union with prior data exports.

In this recipe, we'll use a special type of union that is part of the input step, rather than a step by itself. Using the **Union** functionality during input allows you to ingest and union multiple input files simultaneously.

## Getting ready

To follow along with this recipe, download the `Sample Files 5.2` folder from this book's GitHub repository. This folder contains sales data that has been exported every month, and so we have one file for every month of the year 2016, 12 files in total, to be combined using a union.

## How to do it...

Start by opening Tableau Prep and perform the following steps to create a dynamic input and union step:

1.  Connect to the `January 2016 Sales.xlsx` Excel file in order to create a brand-new flow with a data connection.

2. From the available tables, drag the `Sales_Data` table onto the flow canvas. Then, select the input step in order to display the bottom pane. From the pane, select **Multiple Files**, followed by **Wildcard union**:

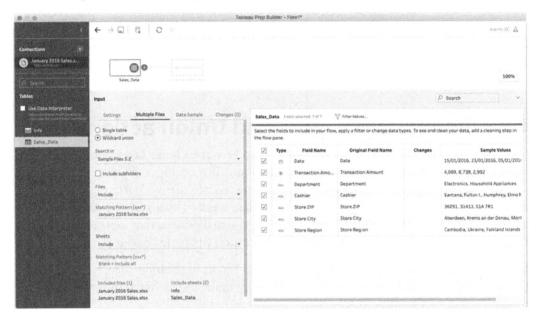

Figure 5.9 – Selecting Wildcard union from the Input options in the bottom pane

**Wildcard union** allows you to perform a union within the input data connection. That is, you can union multiple files at the same time. Wildcards, represented by the asterisk, *, symbol, are utilized to refer to any number of files in a given directory that match a certain naming pattern.

In this recipe, we will perform a union to combine all 12 Excel files in the sample folder.

3. By default, **Matching Pattern** is identical to the filename of the current connection, in this case, `January 2016 Sales.xlsx`. To capture all files in the directory, we can replace any number of characters using a wildcard. Set **Matching Pattern** to `*2016 Sales.xlsx`. This will instruct Tableau Prep to include every file ending in `2016 Sales.xlsx`. In this example, we've replaced the month with a wildcard, and hence all 12 files are now in scope.

4.  Once you've set the **Matching Pattern** field, Tableau Prep will immediately scan the files in scope, and identify the sheet names per file. You will be presented with a full list of file and sheet names under **Sheets**. Notice how each file from our sample data contains two sheets, Sales_Data and Info:

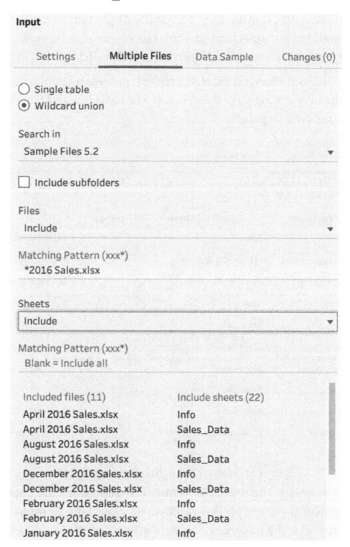

Figure 5.10 – Reviewing the available sheets

The data we want to capture resides in the Sales_Data sheet. As such, we need to provide a matching pattern for sheets, so that only the sheet carrying that name will be included. Since the sheet names are identical, we can achieve this without a wildcard.

Note that we can set our **Matching Pattern** behavior to **Include** or **Exclude**. Using the dropdown highlighted in *Figure 5.10*, by setting this option to **Exclude**, you can specify the **Matching Pattern** value as Info. In doing so, you're instructing Tableau Prep to exclude all sheets named Info.

5.  To confirm the settings, make sure to click the **Apply** button at the bottom of the pane. Depending on your screen size, this button may not be visible initially. Scroll down to the bottom to reveal the **Apply** button and click it.

6.  After applying your changes, Tableau Prep will provide a list of field names found across all the files in scope. Furthermore, it will provide us with a preview of values per field in the bottom pane:

**Sales_Data**  Fields selected: 10 of 10   ▽ Filter Values...

Select the fields to include in your flow, apply a filter or change data types. To see and clean your data, add a cleaning step in the flow pane.

| ☑ | Type | Field Name | Original Field Name | Changes | Sample Values |
|---|---|---|---|---|---|
| ☑ | 📅 | Date | Date | | 08/04/2016, 05/04/2016, 22/04/201 |
| ☑ | # | Transaction Amo... | Transaction Amount | | 3,433, 2,554, 3,082 |
| ☑ | Abc | Department | Department | | Groceries, Household Appliances, Ele |
| ☑ | Abc | Cashier | Cashier | | Sharpe, Tasha F., Cooke, Philip R., Gr |
| ☑ | Abc | Store ZIP | Store ZIP | | 69993, 7584, 10105 |
| ☑ | Abc | Store City | Store City | | Neerheylissem, Machilipatnam, Fort |
| ☑ | Abc | Store Region | Store Region | | South Africa, Mexico, Nauru |
| ☑ | # | Revenue | Revenue | | null |
| ☑ | Abc | Table Names | Table Names | | Sales_Data |
| ☑ | Abc | File Paths | File Paths | | April 2016 Sales.xlsx |

Figure 5.11 – Sales_Data preview after input union

Notice that there is a field named **Revenue** with null values. Throughout this book, we've used these sample files multiple times and the **Revenue** field name is unexpected, as is the null value. To investigate this further, add a clean step to your flow.

7.  With **Clean 1** selected, scroll through the field list, to the **Revenue** field. The data profile shows a large number of null values, confirming our suspicion that there's something not right here. Select the `null` value in the profile chart. Doing so will highlight the origins of the `null` value in the **File Paths** field, which has automatically been added by Tableau Prep, as a result of the union. Here, we can clearly see that null values are present in all files, except the `November 2016 Sales.xlsx` file:

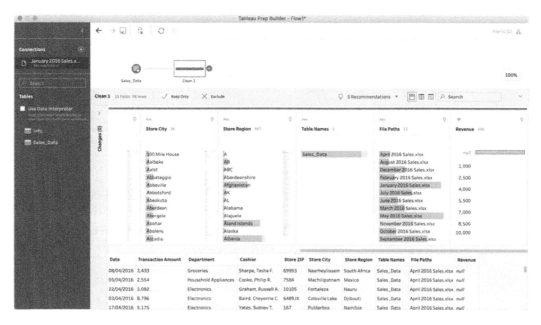

Figure 5.12 – Investigating the Revenue null origins with a data profile

8.  The only other numeric field in the dataset is **Transaction Amount**, so it is worth investigating that field as well. When you scroll over to the **Transaction Amount** field, you'll once again see a significant number of `null` values. Repeat the process from the previous step, select the `null` value, and then observe the origins in the **File Paths** field.

    This time, you can see that the origin is the opposite. All `null` values originate from the `November 2016 Sales.xlsx` file. And so we have determined that **Transaction Amount** and **Revenue** are likely to represent the same data, but the field labels have changed in the November file.

9.  To resolve the problem we have identified, we need to merge the **Transaction Amount** and **Revenue** fields into a single field. To do so, select the **Transaction Amount** field, press the *Ctrl* key, and then select the **Revenue** field as well. With both fields selected, open the options menu on either field and then select **Merge**:

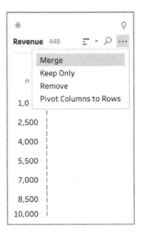

Figure 5.13 – The Merge option will appear when multiple fields are selected

Tableau Prep will instantly merge the fields and assign it the name of the field first selected. An icon above that field will indicate the merge action. Hovering over the icon provides details on the fields that were merged:

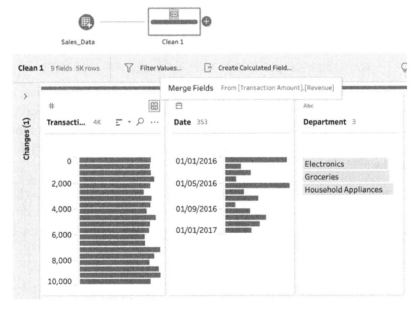

Figure 5.14 – Hovering over the merge icon to see the fields included in the merge

With these steps completed, you have successfully performed a union during the input step.

## How it works...

Tableau Prep stacks rows from data files in scope, as defined by matching patterns during its data ingestion. It does so by opening up multiple files in the background and stacking them without any significant controls in place. That is, completely different data sources can be combined in this union, leading to undesirable outcomes. We've seen a brief example of this in this recipe, where only a single field mismatch justified an investigation.

However, if you are confident that the data format is consistent, as is often the case with automated processes, for example, the input wildcard union option is a great way to ingest files dynamically. For example, a folder that is updated every day with a new file carrying the current date can be included by Tableau Prep thanks to the input wildcard union support.

In this recipe, we've created a union as part of the input step, leveraged a filename and sheet matching pattern, toggled the matching style from include to exclude, and investigated a discrepancy as a result of a union of files with a different structure. As a result, we've learned how to ingest multiple files and perform a Union action using a single input step.

# Combining datasets using an inner join

We often store in multiple different places for a variety of reasons, including different systems, storage optimization and efficiency, security, costs, and so forth. When analyzing data, however, we often want to bring data from many different areas together to create a richer dataset for analysis. Doing so may result in a better understanding of the data and provide valuable business insights. We can use the **Join** functionality to combine data horizontally, that is, widen the dataset by adding fields from two or more sources together. There are a variety of different join types, as you can see by the recipes in this chapter. In this recipe, we'll look at creating an **inner join**.

An inner join is the end result of joining two data sources together and retaining only those rows that overlap. For example, let's assume we have order data for a B2B seller of office supplies. Their data may be segmented into a database containing order information, and another database containing customer information. The overlap between these two sources is a common identifier, such as the customer's name, or, more likely, a unique customer ID.

# Getting ready

To follow along with this recipe, download the `Sample Files 5.3` folder from this book's GitHub repository.

# How to do it...

Start by opening Tableau Prep and perform the following steps to combine the two sample files using the **Inner Join** functionality:

1.  Connect to the `Orders.csv` text file in order to create a brand-new flow with a data connection. The `Orders` file contains order data from a B2B supplier. Each row represents a separate order. Each customer is denoted by a unique identifier in the **cust_id** field:

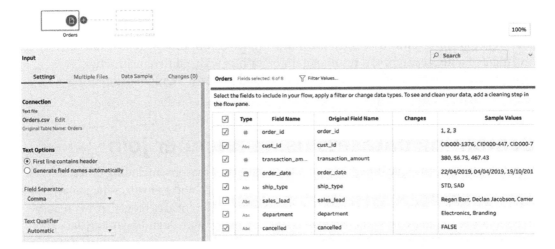

Figure 5.15 – The cust_id field is a unique identifier, essential to the join operation

2.  In our sample data folder, there is a separate file containing customer details, such as a customer contact name, email, and geographic information. In order to perform a comprehensive analysis on orders, for example, identifying the total sales by `State` or `County`, we need to combine these datasets. To get started, create a second connection in your flow to the `Customers.csv` file.

3.  In order to start any new **join**, whether that is an inner join or any other type, we need to click and drag the second data connection step over the first step. When you hover on top of the first connection step, two options will appear, **Union** and **Join**. Ensure that **Join** is highlighted and then release your mouse hold:

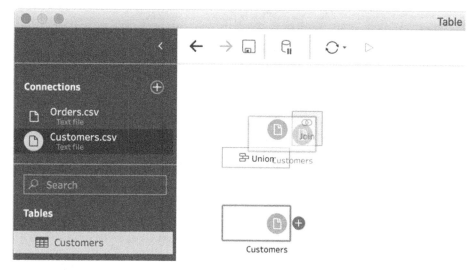

Figure 5.16 – Creating a new join by dropping an input step on top of another input step

A join will always require additional configuration before it is ready for use. Because Tableau Prep instantly evaluates the validity of your flow, creating a new join will initially result in a warning message. This is expected behavior and nothing to be concerned about:

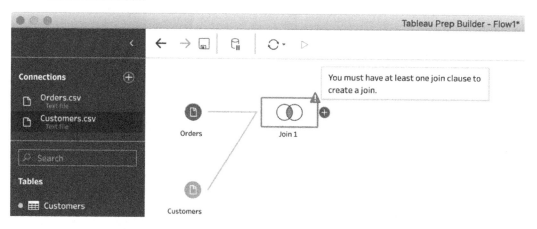

Figure 5.17 – A new join will trigger a warning message

4.  Next, we need to specify how these two data sources can be connected, that is, which field, or combination of fields, they have in common. We can specify this in the bottom pane, in the **Applied Join Clauses** section. Here, click **Add** to reveal two field name lists. The field name lists indicate their source data connection, **Orders** and **Customers**, just above the search bar:

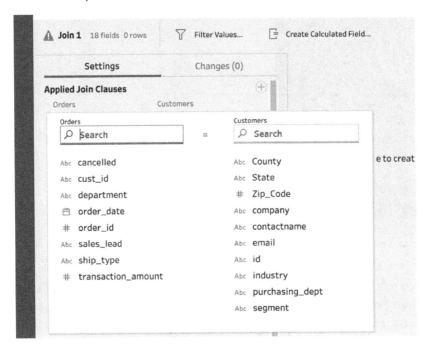

Figure 5.18 – Specifying a new join clause

These data sources are connected by customer ID. In the **Orders** data source, this field is denoted by **cust_id**. In the **Customers** data source, it is denoted by **id**. Select these two fields to create your join clause.

Once a join clause has been created, as we did in the previous step, Tableau Prep will immediately execute the join and provide detailed results in the bottom pane. There are two specific areas to pay careful attention to when creating a join, **Join Type** and **Summary of Join Results**.

**Join Type** allows us to set the type of join, that is, an inner, left, right, full outer, or other type of join. By default, the type is set to **inner**, which is the type we require in this recipe, and so we do not have to alter it. An inner join will return all data that overlaps between the two data sources; in our case, all orders that have a customer associated with them.

In the following screenshot, we can see that the overlapping section of the two circles is selected, resulting in **Join Type : inner**:

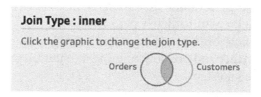

Figure 5.19 – The default join type is inner

**Summary of Join Results** provides valuable information regarding the outcome of a join operation. Specifically, it will inform us how many records are returned from each data source, after passing through the join, and how many records did not pass through because of a mismatch. In our example, a mismatch would occur if an order would *not* have a customer associated with it in the Customers.csv file. Our sample data has not mismatched and we're seeing a total of 15,821 rows from the Orders file passed through the join, as well as 1,467 rows from the Customers file. You can open both files in Excel to confirm that this is indeed the correct number of rows.

The following screenshot shows the join results of the steps we have just performed:

**Summary of Join Results**

Click the bar segments to view the included and excluded values.

////  Mismatched values

|            | Included |
|------------|----------|
| Orders     | 15,821   |
| Customers  | 1,467    |
| Join Result | 15,821  |

Figure 5.20 – Using Summary of Join Results to verify the join operation outcome

Let's move on to the next section!

## How it works...

In this recipe, you've connected two data sources in a Tableau Prep flow. You then joined these two data sources using a common denominator, in this case, the customer ID. You've experienced how Tableau Prep immediately performs join operations without the need for you to run the entire flow. This is by design, and helps you validate your join prior to building out your flow further and possibly running into unexpected issues later on as a result of the output of the join step.

# Combining datasets using a left or right join

In the *Combining datasets using an inner join* recipe, we combined data that was complementary and complete, orders, and associated customer information. However you may find a use case where complementary data is present for some records, and not for others. An example of this that we'll use in this recipe involves two data sources, one with sales data from a department store, and another data source with information from customers who checked out with a loyalty card. Of course, not all customers may have a loyalty card, and so we cannot expect to match every row in the data. This is where a **left join** comes into play.

In a left join, we pass through all the data from the first dataset, that is, the left data source, and only those records from the second, right data source that we were able to match. This means that any sales records that did not involve a loyalty card will still pass through, but the additional fields from the second source will simply be empty, or null.

## Getting ready

To follow along with this recipe, download the `Sample Files 5.4` folder from this book's GitHub repository.

## How to do it...

Start by opening Tableau Prep and perform the following steps to enrich the sample sales data with the customer loyalty card data, if available:

1. Connect to the `Sales Data.xlsx` Excel file in order to create a brand-new flow with a data connection. Let's assume this is sales data from a checkout system, where a customer may or may not have used a loyalty card. If the transaction involved a loyalty card, there will be a value in the `Loyalty_ID` field, otherwise it will be null.

2. Now, bring in the customer loyalty card data by creating a second data connection, this time to the `LoyaltyData.csv` text file.

3.  Create a join by dragging the **LoyaltyData** data source on top of the **Sales Data** source, ensuring that you release when the join is highlighted:

Figure 5.21 – The initial step for creating any type of join is dropping one source on top of another

4.  Set the join clause to use the **Loyalty_ID** field from the **Sales Data** source and the **ID** field from the **LoyaltyData** source. Once you apply the join clause, Tableau Prep will immediately perform the join operation and, after a few moments, provide you with the results, in both summary and detail, within the bottom pane:

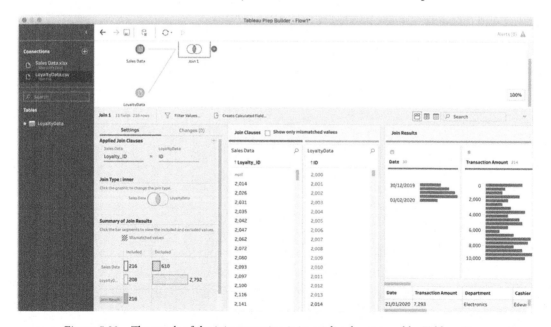

Figure 5.22 – The result of the join operation is immediately returned by Tableau Prep

Note that Tableau Prep indicates a number of mismatched values in the **Summary of Join Results** section. Because the default join type is an inner join, Tableau Prep will only return rows that have a common identifier in both sources, in this case, our loyalty ID. Any other rows are excluded. The join result gives the count of rows that actually passed through the join, 216 in this case, out of a total of 826 sales transactions:

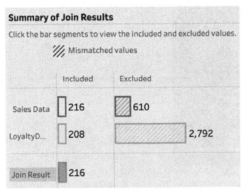

Figure 5.23 – Reviewing the result of your join in the summary section

The middle section in the join step settings shows all the IDs that could not be matched in a red font. For example, **null** from **Sales Data** could not be matched to any row in the **LoyaltyData** file and, as a result, is excluded from the join results. Similarly, the ID **2000** from the **LoyaltyData** file was not present in the sales data, and therefore is also excluded from the join results:

| Join Clauses ☐ Show only mismatched values | |
|---|---|
| **Sales Data** 🔍 | **LoyaltyData** 🔍 |
| ↑ **Loyalty_ID** | ↑ **ID** |
| *null* | 2,000 |
| 2,014 | 2,001 |
| 2,026 | 2,002 |
| 2,031 | 2,003 |
| 2,035 | 2,004 |
| 2,042 | 2,005 |
| 2,047 | 2,006 |
| 2,062 | 2,007 |
| 2,072 | 2,008 |
| 2,080 | 2,009 |
| 2,093 | 2,010 |
| 2,097 | 2,011 |
| 2,100 | 2,012 |
| 2,116 | 2,013 |
| 2,141 | 2,014 |

Figure 5.24 – You can review the excluded details by focusing on the items in red

5.  In our case, we want to return all our sales data rows and simply augment them with loyalty card data, if the customer used a loyalty card. Therefore, we need to change our join type to **Left Join**, meaning that we want to retrieve all data from the left side, Sales Data, and only those rows from the right side, LoyaltyData, when there is an overlap, based on Loyalty ID. To change the join type, select the left circle in the **Join Type** Venn diagram:

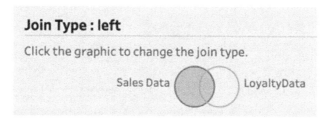

Figure 5.25 – Click the left circle to change the join type to a left join

Tableau Prep immediately updates the join results, and, at a glance, we can now see from the summary that all 826 Sales Data rows are being passed through:

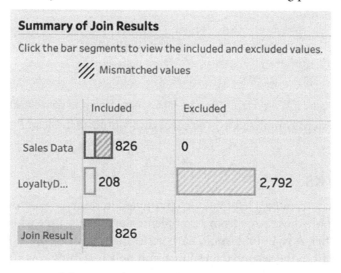

Figure 5.26 – A left join results in no values being excluded from the left side

You may review the row-by-row results in a more organized pane by adding a clean step to your flow and selecting **null** from the **Loyalty_ID** field. This will display all rows where a transaction was made without a loyalty card, and you can see that the values for customer information are set to **null** as a result:

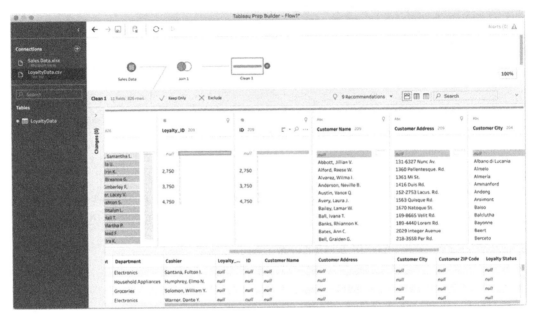

Figure 5.27 – A clean step is useful for inspecting your data quickly

With these steps completed, you've successfully utilized Tableau Prep to perform a left join.

## How it works...

In this recipe, you've created a left join, which resulted in returning all rows from one data source, and only those rows from a complementary data source when there was a common identifier. A right join would have performed the exact opposite, that is, returned all rows from the second data source, and only matching rows from the first data source.

There are many use cases for a left or right join, as in many scenarios we combine data from multiple sources to a core data source, such as transactions or customers.

# Expanding datasets using a full outer join

In the *Combining data ingest and Union actions* recipe, we created an inner join to return rows from two data sources that had a commonality. In the *Combining datasets using a left or right join* recipe, we created a left join to return all rows from a data source and enrich that data with information from a second source, whenever there was additional information available, without dropping any rows from the original source.

In this recipe, we'll look at a variation of the join, which is named the **full outer join**. In this case, we'll want to retrieve all rows from both data sources involved in the join, that is, even if there's no overlap. It's essentially doing a left and right join at the same time; you won't lose any data from either data source.

In the example that follows, we'll use a use case where a company is running several projects and each project may have a number of people assigned to it. However, some projects may not have started yet, or may have already been completed. Those inactive projects won't have people assigned to them. Similarly, people may be assigned to a project, or are currently between projects and not assigned directly to any project. We want the result of our join to return all projects and all people.

## Getting ready

To follow along with this recipe, download the `Sample Files 5.5` folder from this book's GitHub repository.

## How to do it...

Start by opening Tableau Prep and perform the following steps to create a full outer join to combine project and people data:

1.  Connect to the `Projects.xlsx` Excel file in order to create a brand-new flow with a data connection. From the available tables, drag the **Projects** table onto the canvas.

2.  The source we've connected to contains two tables, **Projects** and **Project Staff**. Without creating a brand-new data connection, drag the **Project Staff** table onto the canvas to create a second input, using the same data connection:

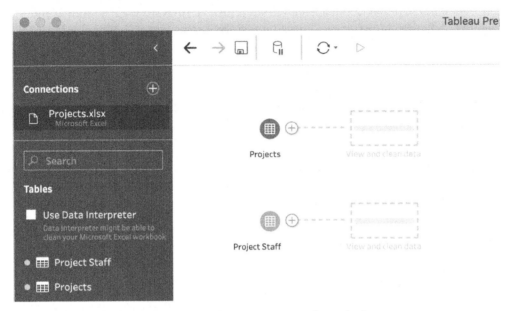

Figure 5.28 – Using the same connection for multiple inputs

3.  To initiate the join creation process, drag the **Project Staff** input on top of **Projects**, releasing it when the join icon is highlighted.

4.  Create a join clause using the **Project Name** field for the **Projects** input, and the **Project** field for the **Project Staff** input.

5.  To complete the configuration, click the left circle in the Venn diagram, followed by the right circle. This will then update the join to become a full outer join. Notice that the type name is abbreviated to simply state **full**:

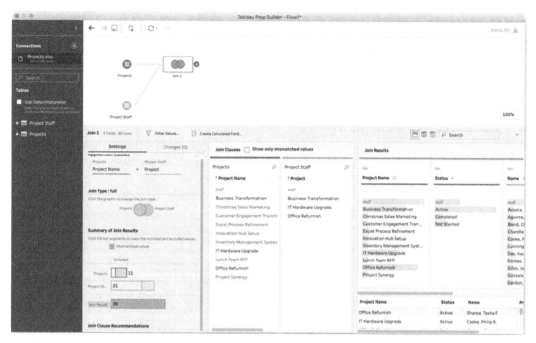

Figure 5.29 – A complete full outer join may show many mismatched values

With these steps completed, you've successfully performed a full outer join with Tableau Prep.

## How it works...

In this recipe, you've leveraged a full outer join to combine two data sources, even if those sources have nothing in common. In this case, we have included projects that were not assigned any staff and included staff that were not assigned to any project.

Using a full outer join can come in handy for specific scenarios. However, there is a risk of creating a dataset that is incorrect since, with a full outer join, you may expect many mismatched values, and a mistake is easily made by ignoring the mismatches. It is prudent to double-check that your join clause is correct with any join, but perhaps even more so with a full join, for this reason.

# Expanding datasets using a not inner join

In this chapter, we have assumed in all join-related recipes that there was an overlap between two data sources. However, for analysis purposes, you may be interested in what data is not overlapping, so that you can take action appropriately.

Using the same data as we've used in the *Expanding datasets using a full outer join* recipe, where we have a data source with projects, and another data source with project staff, we may change our use case to focus solely on data that does not overlap. That is, we are only interested in projects without staff assigned to them, or staff members not currently assigned to work on any project.

## Getting ready

To follow along with this recipe, download the `Sample Files 5.6` folder from this book's GitHub repository.

## How to do it...

Start by opening Tableau Prep and perform the following steps to create a **not inner join**:

1. Connect to the `Projects.xlsx` Excel file in order to create a brand-new flow with a data connection. From the available tables, drag **Projects** onto the canvas.

2. From the same list of tables, drag **Project Staff** onto the canvas to create a second input step.

3. Drag the **Project Staff** step on top of **Projects**, releasing when the join icon is highlighted, in order to create a new join.

4. Configure **Join Clause** to match the data on **Project Name** from the **Projects** source, and **Project** from the **Project Staff** source.

5.  To create the **not inner join**, click the Venn diagram in the following order. First, click the left circle, then the right circle, and finally the center where both circles overlap. When done, the join type will state **notInner**:

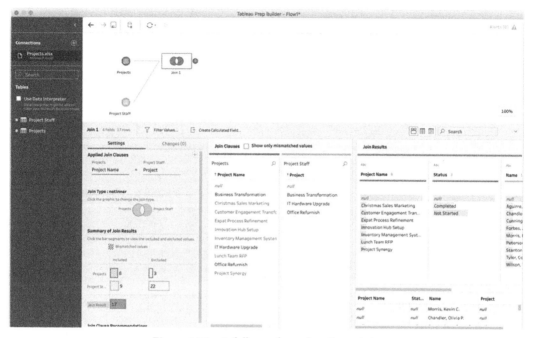

Figure 5.30 – A fully configured notInner join

6.  Add a clean step to your flow, after the join, to view the data in the preview section. Here, you can clearly see that you have included only projects without staff and staff without projects:

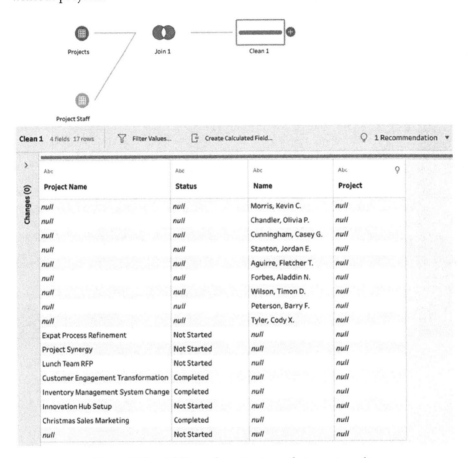

| Project Name | Status | Name | Project |
|---|---|---|---|
| *null* | *null* | Morris, Kevin C. | *null* |
| *null* | *null* | Chandler, Olivia P. | *null* |
| *null* | *null* | Cunningham, Casey G. | *null* |
| *null* | *null* | Stanton, Jordan E. | *null* |
| *null* | *null* | Aguirre, Fletcher T. | *null* |
| *null* | *null* | Forbes, Aladdin N. | *null* |
| *null* | *null* | Wilson, Timon D. | *null* |
| *null* | *null* | Peterson, Barry F. | *null* |
| *null* | *null* | Tyler, Cody X. | *null* |
| Expat Process Refinement | Not Started | *null* | *null* |
| Project Synergy | Not Started | *null* | *null* |
| Lunch Team RFP | Not Started | *null* | *null* |
| Customer Engagement Transformation | Completed | *null* | *null* |
| Inventory Management System Change | Completed | *null* | *null* |
| Innovation Hub Setup | Not Started | *null* | *null* |
| Christmas Sales Marketing | Completed | *null* | *null* |
| *null* | Not Started | *null* | *null* |

Figure 5.31 – Adding a clean step to easily inspect results

With this step completed, you've performed the **Not Inner Join** method of discarding data.

## How it works...

A not inner join works by discarding the data which would be put through as the result of an inner join. In doing so, Tableau Prep allows you to quickly identify rows that cannot be matched across the data sources used. This can be helpful in scenarios such as the one used in this recipe, or even for identifying data quality issues where you expect a match, but the data is not providing a match on every row.

# 6
# Pivoting Data

You may encounter a scenario where analyzing data is complicated by the way the data is structured. For example, you may prefer to have columns as rows or vice versa. For example, you may have a column in your dataset with a true/false value for each product category. However, your data visualization would be easier to achieve if you had a single column for the product category, with the row value indicating the category name. In this chapter, you'll learn how to pivot your data from columns to rows and vice versa. The goal of pivoting is to ensure your data has the optimal shape required for your downstream analytics goals, for example, creating a dashboard in Tableau Desktop. Mastering the pivot functionality is an essential tool in your data transformation skillset.

In this chapter, you'll find the following recipes to help you pivot your data for analytics:

- Pivoting columns to rows
- Pivoting columns to rows using wildcards
- Pivoting rows to columns

## Technical requirements

To follow along with the recipes in this chapter, you will need **Tableau Prep Builder**.

The recipes in this chapter use sample data files that you can download from the book's GitHub repository: `https://github.com/PacktPublishing/Tableau-Prep-Cookbook`.

# Pivoting columns to rows

Data is often produced by systems in what the engineers building the system thought was the most efficient manner. Rarely do data processing and storage systems store data with visualization in mind. Similarly, you may have data available that is appropriate for one type of visualization but not another. In this recipe, we'll look at a sales dataset. This dataset has sales revenue values per category. The categories are `Electronics`, `Groceries`, and `Household Appliances`. Each of the categories has its own column, which prevents us from easily making a line chart with overall revenue. To resolve this, we're going to pivot the data such that these three individual columns become a single `Category` column, and values are placed in a single `Revenue` column.

## Getting ready

To follow along with this recipe, download the `Sample Files 6.1` folder from this book's GitHub repository.

## How to do it...

Start by opening the `Sales Data.csv` file from the `Sample Files 6.1` folder in **Tableau Prep**, then follow the steps to pivot the data:

1.  Add a **Clean** step and expand the bottom pane, to get a preview of the data:

| Groceries | Electronics | Household Appliances | Order Date | Sales Person | Store ZIP | Store City | Store Region |
|---|---|---|---|---|---|---|---|
| null | null | 3,391 | 01/12/2016 | Valentine, Ivor W. | 93170-944 | Iseyin | Oyo |
| null | null | 4,527 | 27/12/2016 | Wilkins, Ella X. | 49661 | Mount Isa | QLD |
| null | null | 1,438 | 16/12/2016 | Simmons, Ciaran Q. | 674093 | Sint-Amandsberg | Oost-Vlaanderen |
| null | 2,637 | null | 11/12/2016 | Cortez, Karina C. | 116270 | La Florida | Metropolitana de |
| null | null | 4,331 | 01/12/2016 | Dawson, Quyn L. | 707613 | Dos Hermanas | AN |
| null | null | 756 | 11/12/2016 | Roach, Kitra G. | 4982 | Ramagundam | Andhra Pradesh |
| 56 | null | null | 20/12/2016 | Bean, Nerea I. | 515328 | Telde | Canarias |
| 2,665 | null | null | 25/12/2016 | Matthews, Stephen F | 68951Z | Alajuela | A |
| 7,400 | null | null | 01/12/2016 | Bowman, Nigel I. | 1502 | Baie-Comeau | Quebec |
| null | null | 3,757 | 17/12/2016 | Mccoy, Fritz L. | 42570 | LaSalle | Ontario |
| null | 9,180 | null | 12/12/2016 | Benson, Robin E. | 657373 | Galway | Connacht |
| null | 5,522 | null | 29/12/2016 | Sexton, Hayes A. | 3122LR | Gliwice | Slaskie |
| null | null | 323 | 23/12/2016 | Hyde, Angela R. | 70610 | Istanbul | Istanbul |
| 3,927 | null | null | 21/12/2016 | Mccall, Gareth U. | 34805 | Vienna | Wie |

Figure 6.1 – Inspect the data prior to pivoting

Notice how the first three columns have many null values. You may inspect the data to find that for each row, only one of these columns has a value. In this dataset, the columns represent the product category, and the value is the amount of revenue from the sale.

2.  Click the + symbol on the **Clean 1** step and select **Pivot**, in order to add a **Pivot** step to your flow:

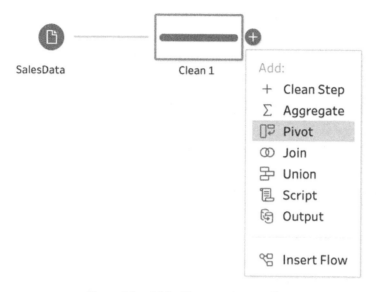

Figure 6.2 – Add a Pivot step to your flow

3.  Select the **Pivot** step and expand the bottom pane to clearly view all content. Take note of the **Pivoted Fields** section. This is where you can drag columns, from the **Fields** list on the left, that you'd like to pivot:

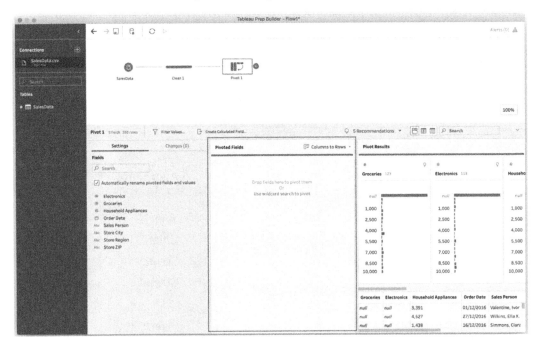

Figure 6.3 – The Pivoted Fields section is where you drag columns to pivot

4.  From the **Fields** list, drag and drop **Electronics**, **Groceries**, and **Household Appliances** onto the **Pivoted Fields** section. In the following screenshot, notice how the **Pivot Results** section is instantly updated with two new fields. The **Pivot 1 Names** field contains the former column names, **Electronics**, **Groceries**, and **Household Appliances**. The **Pivot 1 Values** field contains the values of the three former columns:

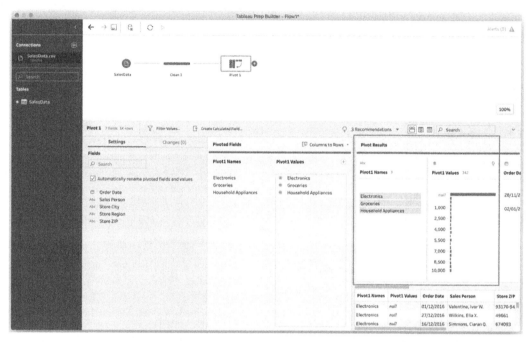

Figure 6.4 – A Columns to Rows pivot will always output two new fields

5. Add a **Clean** step, then rename the **Pivot 1 Names** field Product Category and rename the **Pivot 1 Values** field Revenue. You can double-click the field name in the **Pivot Results** section in order to rename a field.

Toggle between steps **Clean 1** and **Clean 2** and observe the row count in the top-left corner of the bottom pane. Note that the row count was **350** at **Clean 1** and has increased to **1K** rows in **Clean 2**, which can be seen in the following screenshot:

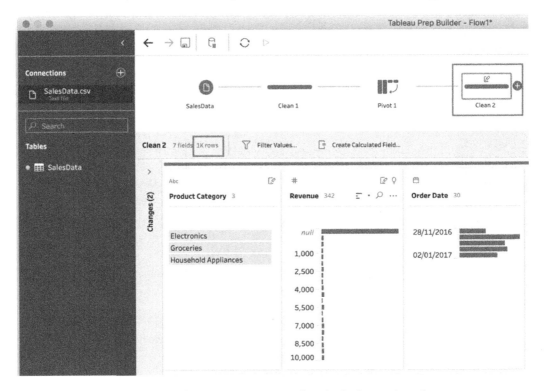

Figure 6.5 – A Columns to Rows pivot will multiply the number of rows
by the number of columns pivoted

To investigate this increase in row count, search for **Valentine** in the **Sales Person** field, then select the name **Valentine Ivor W** in order to filter the data to just this person.

The data preview section will now show us three rows, two of which have no value for **Revenue**. This is the result of the **Pivot** step, which creates a new row for each column we pivot. In our example, we are pivoting three columns and hence have gotten three rows per source row in return, as seen in the following screenshot:

Figure 6.6 – Investigate the row count difference by focusing on a single salesperson

6.  To maintain our data integrity, we need to remove rows where **Revenue** is **null**. To do this, deselect **Valentine** by clicking the name once. Then right-click the **null** values bar in the **Revenue** field and select **Exclude**:

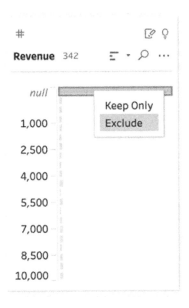

Figure 6.7 – Exclude null values in the pivot values Revenue field

After the exclusion has been applied, notice how the row count is once again 350, matching our source input row count.

## How it works...

In this recipe, we learned how to pivot data. Pivoting data helps prepare your data analysis and is particularly useful when creating reports. When pivoting columns to rows, Tableau Prep creates a new row for each column you selected to pivot, plus two additional columns, one for names and one for values. And so, if you pivot 5 fields in a dataset with 10 fields and 100 rows, the output will be 500 rows (5 columns pivoted multiplied by the number of rows). At the same time, your output will have 7 fields (10 source fields, minus the 5 pivoted fields, plus the 2 additional columns resulting from the pivot).

Since Tableau Prep is not aware of the data context, this may introduce a data challenge for you, as we've seen in the example in the *How to do it...* section, where many rows held a **Revenue** value of **null**. To correct this, you may need to filter your data to remove unwanted rows.

# Pivoting columns to rows using wildcards

If your data is subject to changes over time, particularly the introduction of new columns, your flow may not produce the output expected or even produce an error. When scheduling a flow for recurring execution, it is important that you can rely on its execution being successful. One of the ways in which the **Pivot** function can achieve this goal is by using **wildcards**. Wildcards can be used to identify columns that need to be pivoted, based on a header pattern, rather than an exact match. In this recipe, we'll pivot columns to rows using wildcards.

## Getting ready

To follow along with this recipe, download the `Sample Files 6.2` folder from this book's GitHub repository.

## How to do it...

Start by opening the `SalesData.csv` file from the `Sample Files 6.2` folder in **Tableau Prep**, then follow these steps to pivot columns to rows using wildcards:

1. Add a **Clean** step to your flow, then expand the bottom pane to observe the data preview:

| Cat_Groceries | Cat_Electronics | Cat_Household Appliances | Order Date | Sales Person | Store ZIP | Store City | Store Region |
|---|---|---|---|---|---|---|---|
| *null* | *null* | 3,391 | 01/12/2016 | Valentine, Ivor W. | 93170-944 | Iseyin | Oyo |
| *null* | *null* | 4,527 | 27/12/2016 | Wilkins, Ella X. | 49661 | Mount Isa | QLD |
| *null* | *null* | 1,438 | 16/12/2016 | Simmons, Ciaran Q. | 674093 | Sint-Amandsberg | Oost-Vlaanderen |
| *null* | 2,637 | *null* | 11/12/2016 | Cortez, Karina C. | 116270 | La Florida | Metropolitana de Santiago |
| *null* | *null* | 4,331 | 01/12/2016 | Dawson, Quyn L. | 707613 | Dos Hermanas | AN |
| *null* | *null* | 756 | 11/12/2016 | Roach, Kitra G. | 4982 | Ramagundam | Andhra Pradesh |
| 56 | *null* | *null* | 20/12/2016 | Bean, Nerea I. | 515328 | Telde | Canarias |
| 2,665 | *null* | *null* | 25/12/2016 | Matthews, Stephen F. | 68951Z | Alajuela | A |

Figure 6.8 – Identify the fields to be transformed in the data preview

> **Important note**
>
> Note that the sales data includes revenue information per **product category**.
> Each category field name is prefixed with **Cat_**. In this example, we have three
> product categories: **Groceries**, **Electronics**, and **Household Appliances**. These
> three categories are shown in our data as **Cat_Groceries**, **Cat_Electronics**, and
> **Cat_Household Appliances**.
>
> Suppose the dataset we connected to only includes a product column when an
> actual sale was made in that product category for the time period that the data
> reflects. That is, if no sales were made for the **Cat_Electronics** category, then
> that category would not appear in our data at all. Because of that, we cannot
> easily pivot, since the **Cat_Electronics** value is not known to Tableau Prep.
> The next time we process this data, fewer or more product category fields may
> appear, including **Cat_Electronics**, and a regular **Pivot** step would not process
> such changes. However, using wildcards allows us to pivot all fields with a
> certain pattern. In our case, we'll look for fields starting with **Cat_**. Doing
> so allows our data to change over time and new categories can be added. As
> long as those categories start with **Cat_**, our flow will be able to process them
> automatically, without the need for us to amend the flow.

2.  Next expand your flow by adding a **Pivot** step. Then, instead of dragging fields into
    the pivot configuration pane, click the **Use wildcard search to pivot** link text:

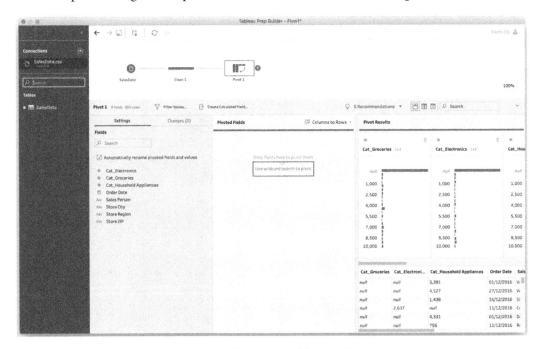

Figure 6.9 – Access the wildcard settings

3. In the wildcard settings, type `Cat1_` in the **Pivot 1 Values** text box and press the *Enter* key:

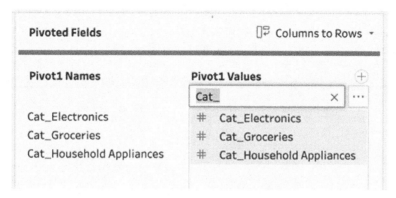

Figure 6.10 – Identify all fields starting with Cat_

You've now performed a wildcard search on the field names in our dataset. And each field including the text `Cat_` is identified and added to the **Pivot** step.

4. Click the ellipsis (...) button next to the wildcard search text and set **Search Options** to **Starts with**:

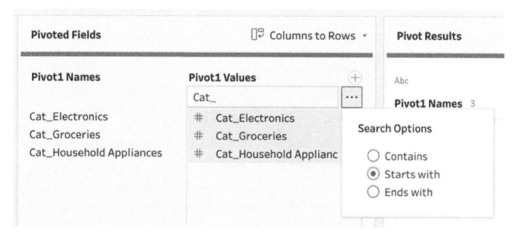

Figure 6.11 – Changing the search options

Setting **Search Options** to **Starts with** will ensure that only field names starting with `Cat_` are included in our pivot. In the unlikely event that our product category includes the characters `Cat_` anywhere else, as part of the category name, such fields will be ignored from now on.

5.  Add a **Clean** step and rename the newly created **Pivot 1 Names** field **Product Category** and rename the **Pivot 1 Values** field **Revenue**.

6.  To verify that our flow is working, open the `SalesData.csv` CSV file in Excel. Then, add three new columns named `RegisterCat_`, `InventoryCat_2021`, and `Cat_Books`. Save and close the file when done:

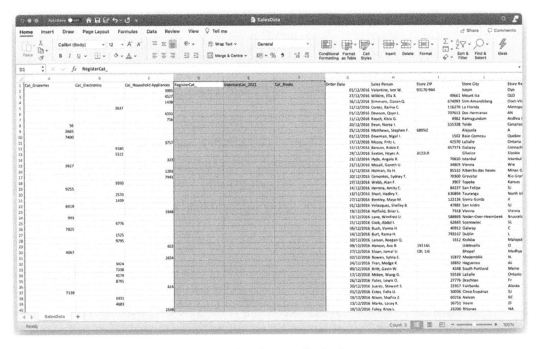

Figure 6.12 – Update the CSV file for this recipe

7.  Close Excel and return to Tableau Prep, then click the **Refresh Data** button in the toolbar to refresh the sample data for the flow.

8.  Select the **Pivot** step and notice that it has been updated with only one new field to pivot, that is, the `Cat_Books` field. This is the wildcard pivot in action using the **Starts with** option we set in *Step 4*:

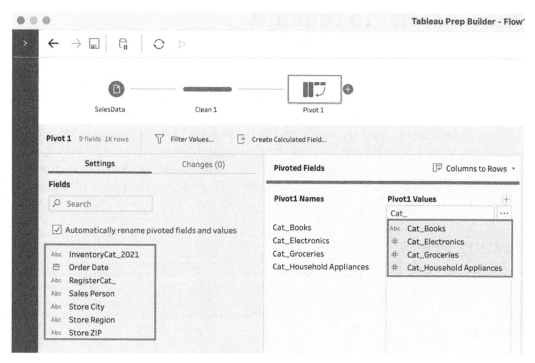

Figure 6.13 – New fields starting with Cat_ are automatically included

Let's move on to the next section!

## How it works...

In this recipe, we learned how to leverage wildcards to create a more dynamic flow. Doing so allows your flow to handle changes in your data as they occur. When pivoting columns to rows in Tableau Prep, Tableau Prep relies on fixed input from the user to specify exactly which columns to pivot. With the wildcard option, Tableau has added flexibility here. Instead of specifying the exact column name, Tableau Prep will include all columns that either include, start with, or end with certain text, as specified by you. This allows you to have a dynamic data feed that introduces or removes fields over time and allows your flow to handle such changes without complications.

# Pivoting rows to columns

When preparing data that has been generated by transactional systems, you may encounter data structures that appear nonsensical from a reporting and analytics perspective. Take a sales order as an example. A sale may be for one or multiple items and the total sales amount may be affected by things such as a loyalty card, discount, referral code, and of course sales tax. Depending on which system you are working with, such information may be reported separately, that is, in columns. However, it's quite likely to see multiple rows in your dataset for the same transaction. In this recipe, we'll look at pivoting data from rows to columns, which will resolve any issues arising from such a data structure. Broadly, these steps are similar to pivoting columns to rows, with some important differences, as we'll see.

## Getting ready

To follow along with this recipe, download the `Sample Files 6.3` folder from this book's GitHub repository.

## How to do it...

Start by opening the `RevenueData.csv` file from the `Sample Files 6.3` folder in **Tableau Prep**, then follow these steps to pivot rows to columns:

1.  Add a **Clean** step to your flow and expand the bottom pane so you can easily inspect the data:

Figure 6.14 – Add a Clean step to inspect your data

We can observe two items of interest in the cleaning step that will confirm our need to apply a pivot transformation, specifically pivoting rows to columns.

Firstly, in the data preview, we can see that **TransactionID** is always repeated: there are two rows with value **1**, two rows with value **2**, two rows with value **3**, and so forth:

| TransactionID | Product Category | LineItem | Value | Order Date | Sales Person | Store ZIP | Store City | Store Region |
|---|---|---|---|---|---|---|---|---|
| 1 | Electronics | Revenue | 2,637 | 11/12/2016 | Cortez, Karina C. | 116270 | La Florida | Metropolitana de Santiago |
| 1 | Electronics | Tax | 131.85 | 11/12/2016 | Cortez, Karina C. | 116270 | La Florida | Metropolitana de Santiago |
| 2 | Electronics | Revenue | 9,180 | 12/12/2016 | Benson, Robin E. | 657373 | Galway | Connacht |
| 2 | Electronics | Tax | 459 | 12/12/2016 | Benson, Robin E. | 657373 | Galway | Connacht |
| 3 | Electronics | Revenue | 5,522 | 29/12/2016 | Sexton, Hayes A. | 3122LR | Gliwice | Slaskie |
| 3 | Electronics | Tax | 276.1 | 29/12/2016 | Sexton, Hayes A. | 3122LR | Gliwice | Slaskie |
| 4 | Electronics | Revenue | 9,350 | 27/12/2016 | Webb, Alan F. | 3907 | Topeka | Kansas |
| 4 | Electronics | Tax | 467.5 | 27/12/2016 | Webb, Alan F. | 3907 | Topeka | Kansas |

Figure 6.15 – The TransactionID values appear to be repeated

Upon further investigation, we can see that there is only one difference between each pair of rows, where a pair is a set of rows with matching **TransactionID** values. That difference is in the **LineItem** field. From the profile pane, we can easily see that there are two distinct values in this field, **Revenue** and **Tax**.

And so we can conclude that one row is the revenue amount for a given transaction, and the other row is the tax amount for that same transaction. In order to make reporting easier, we want to have two columns instead, one for revenue and another for tax. This is where the pivot transformation can help.

2.   Add a **Pivot** step to your flow, then select **Rows to Columns** from the dropdown in the **Pivoted Fields** section:

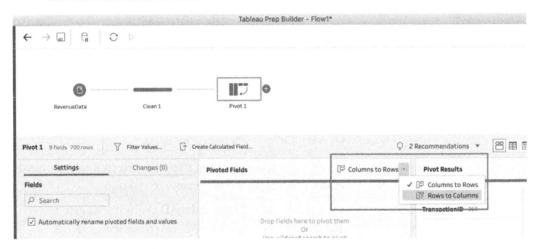

Figure 6.16 – The default pivot setting is Columns to Rows

3.   Next, we need to specify which fields in our data determine the number of columns to add. In our case, we specified that the **LineItem** field holds two values, **Revenue** and **Tax**, which are the values we want as columns. To input this into the pivot configuration, drag the **LineItem** field from the field list, onto the **Pivoted Fields** section. **Tableau Prep** will now scan your dataset for unique values and display them accordingly.

The **Pivot** step in your workflow will now raise an error. This error indicates the pivot configuration is not complete. When it comes to pivoting rows to columns, as opposed to columns to rows, we need to tell **Tableau Prep** which field holds our numeric values.

4.  Drag the **Value** field to the bottom of the **Pivoted Fields** section, titled **Field to Aggregate for new columns**. This completes the configuration:

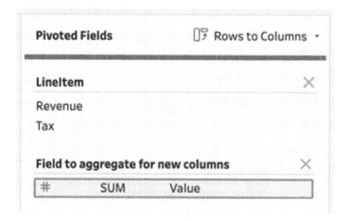

Figure 6.17 – Add the numeric field value for the new columns

Tip

You can change the aggregation at this time from the default **SUM** to any other method. For example, suppose you have student exam test results; you may choose to aggregate using the average, in order to return the average test score per student.

5.  Add another **Clean** step to verify the result of your pivot transformation. Notice how the two new columns, **Revenue** and **Tax**, have been added to the start of your dataset. Also, note how the row count has been reduced from 700 to 350:

Figure 6.18 – Verify your results easily in a Clean step

Let's move on to the next section!

# How it works...

In this recipe, we learned how to pivot rows to columns. This type of pivot may be helpful when your dataset has multiple rows for a single transaction. When pivoting rows to columns in Tableau Prep, Tableau Prep will create as many new columns as there are unique values in the pivot field you specify. Caution is advised here as you may not want to pivot a field with hundreds of unique values and end up with an equal number of new columns.

Secondly, Tableau Prep will populate the values for these columns with another, numeric field that you specify. At this time, Tableau Prep will automatically apply an aggregation operation, by default set to **SUM**. This aggregation is needed as you may have multiple rows with the same unique value.

# 7
# Creating Powerful Calculations

In most analytics scenarios, you'll find that your dataset requires additional calculations in order to perform downstream analysis. For example, you may want to combine the values of multiple fields, or conditionally include certain values only. That's where creating calculated fields comes into play. Calculated fields allow you to perform calculations on your dataset inside Tableau Prep. The benefit of doing so in Tableau Prep rather than in a downstream reporting tool is that Tableau Prep will only need to perform the calculation once. In comparison, if you were to do these calculations in your reports, you'd have to perform them once for each report. Creating a calculation per report requires more effort than creating a calculation once during data preparation. And, of course, if multiple people were to create reports and attempt to calculate a certain value, there would be a risk of applying different calculations, either by mistake or otherwise. These are all great reasons to perform your calculations upstream, in your Tableau Prep flow. In this chapter, we'll cover creating calculated fields during the data preparation part of your analytics flow using Tableau Prep. After completing this chapter, you'll be able to create powerful calculations to enrich your data and ensure all dependent reports can leverage the output of these calculations.

In this chapter, you'll find the following recipes to help you create calculated fields to create a more valuable dataset:

- Creating calculated fields

- Creating conditional calculations

- Extracting substrings

- Changing date formats with calculations

- Creating relative temporal calculations

- Creating regular expressions in calculations

# Technical requirements

To follow along with the recipes in this chapter, you will require **Tableau Prep Builder**.

The recipes in this chapter use sample data files that you can download from the book's GitHub repository: `https://github.com/PacktPublishing/Tableau-Prep-Cookbook`.

# Creating calculated fields

One of the key considerations that is most often overlooked is determining the granularity of the data needed. For example, when working with geographic data, you may have values for the continent, region, country, state, city, ZIP code, street, and so on. But if you only need to report on country data, you may not need all these other dimensions. Or, perhaps you are processing order data; you may want to consider whether you need the details for each individual line item in each individual order, or whether your analysis is satisfied with the total order amount per day. In this recipe, we'll look at a quick method to help reveal the data actually in use in a **Tableau Desktop** visualization.

# Getting ready

To follow along with this recipe, download the `Sample Files 7.1` folder from this book's GitHub repository. There, you'll find the `December 2016 Sales.xlsx` Excel file. In the version of the sales data we've been using throughout this book, you'll find that we have a single field with the subtotal, that is, the amount to be paid for the goods purchased, excluding any applicable taxes or charges. In this recipe, we'll use Tableau Prep to create calculated fields to display the sales tax amount and the total transaction amount, that is, the amount the customer will actually have to pay.

# How to do it...

Start by opening the `December 2016 Sales.xlsx` flow from the `Sample Files 7.1` folder in **Tableau Prep**, then follow these steps:

1.  Examine your dataset and confirm that there is indeed only one numeric field, named **Subtotal**, as shown in the following screenshot:

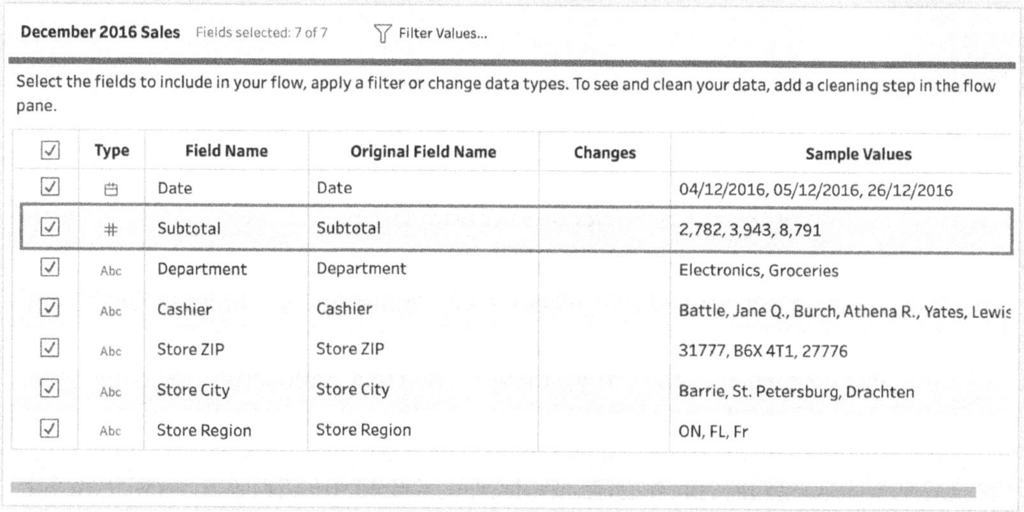

| | Type | Field Name | Original Field Name | Changes | Sample Values |
|---|---|---|---|---|---|
| ✓ | 🗓 | Date | Date | | 04/12/2016, 05/12/2016, 26/12/2016 |
| ✓ | # | Subtotal | Subtotal | | 2,782, 3,943, 8,791 |
| ✓ | Abc | Department | Department | | Electronics, Groceries |
| ✓ | Abc | Cashier | Cashier | | Battle, Jane Q., Burch, Athena R., Yates, Lewis |
| ✓ | Abc | Store ZIP | Store ZIP | | 31777, B6X 4T1, 27776 |
| ✓ | Abc | Store City | Store City | | Barrie, St. Petersburg, Drachten |
| ✓ | Abc | Store Region | Store Region | | ON, FL, Fr |

**December 2016 Sales**    Fields selected: 7 of 7      ⛢ Filter Values...

Select the fields to include in your flow, apply a filter or change data types. To see and clean your data, add a cleaning step in the flow pane.

Figure 7.1 – The dataset only includes the subtotal, not the final transaction amount

2. Click the plus icon on your **December 2016 Sales** step and add a clean step. With the clean step selected, the **Create Calculated Field** button will appear in the bottom pane, as shown in the following screenshot:

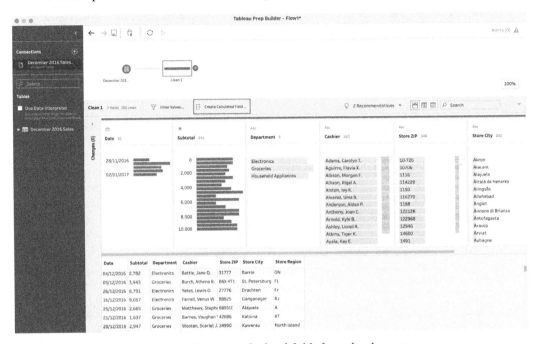

Figure 7.2 – We create calculated fields from the clean step

3. Click the **Create Calculated Field** button to bring up the **Add Field** dialog. This is where we can create and edit calculated fields. At the top, we'll find the **Field Name** input box, as seen in the following screenshot, which is where we can give our calculated field a name. The text we input in the **Field Name** box is the name of the new column that will be added to our dataset. Below that, we find an empty input box. This input box is where we will type our calculations. Finally, below that is the validation status, which currently displays **Calculation is valid**. As we type our calculations, Tableau Prep will validate the calculation in real time and provide hints on any potential calculation issues as they occur:

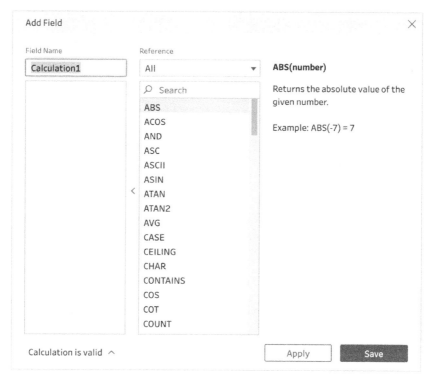

Figure 7.3 – Click Create Calculated Field to open the Add Field dialog

> **Important note**
>
> In the **Add Field** dialog, you can type your calculation from scratch or use the functions listed in the **Reference** list to the right to get started. When selecting an advanced function in the **Reference** list, you will see an explanation of that function to the right.
>
> When you double-click an item in the **Reference** list, it will automatically add a template calculation to the input box to the right so that you can build calculations faster.
>
> The **Reference** list does not include basic arithmetic operations, such as addition or subtraction. Nevertheless, you can use such operators in your calculations.

4.  Let's create a calculated field that will state the total transaction amount the customer has to pay including sales taxes. In this example, let's assume a flat-rate sales tax that is applicable to all goods, set at 6.5%. In order to calculate the total transaction amount, we need to multiply the **Subtotal** field we identified in *Step 1* by 1.065. Get started by setting the field name to Transaction Amount.

5.   Next, in the calculation input box, type in Sub. Notice how Tableau Prep's autocomplete function suggests the **Subtotal** field. Click the suggestion to add it to your calculation:

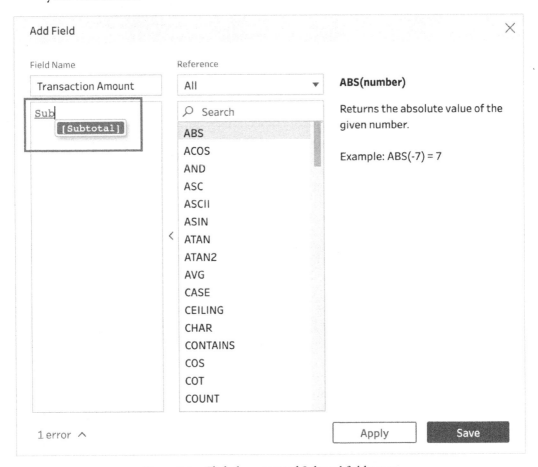

Figure 7.4 – Click the suggested Subtotal field name

6.  In order to multiply **Subtotal** by 1.065, enter `* 1.065` in the calculated field input box and click **Save** to add your new calculated field:

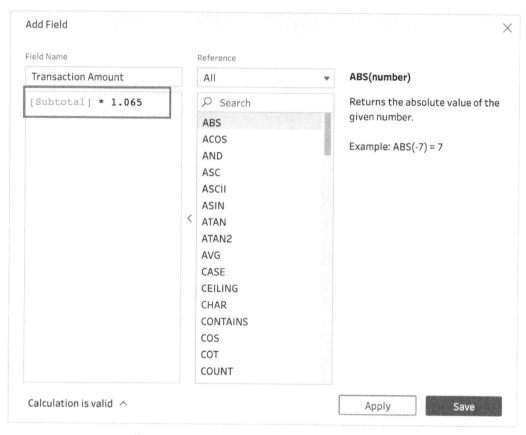

Figure 7.5 – Complete the calculation and click Save

7.  You'll instantly see your newly added **Transaction Amount** field in the field list and the data preview. Newly added calculated fields are added to the beginning. Drag the field so that it's positioned after the **Subtotal** field, as shown in the following screenshot:

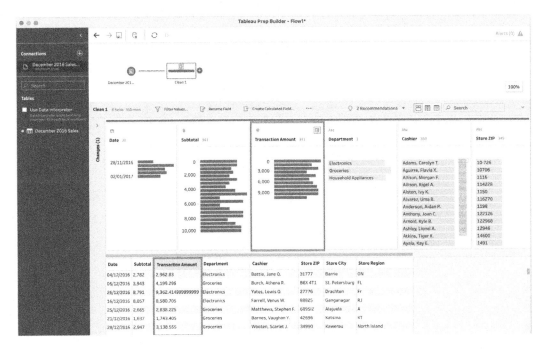

Figure 7.6 – Re-arrange the newly added Sales Tax Amount field

> **Important note**
>
> Although Tableau Prep indicated that the calculation is valid, it only checks for the arithmetic and logic, not whether your calculation outcome is the one you were aiming for. Because Tableau Prep has a handy data preview instantly available to you, I always like to pick up a calculator and calculate the outcome of two or three rows to ensure the outcome is as expected.

8.  Let's practice adding another calculated field, this time to return the sales tax amount. We don't need to add another clean step in order to add another calculated field. You can create multiple calculated fields in a single clean step or across multiple clean steps. With the **Transaction Amount** field still selected, from dragging it to its new position in *Step 7*, click the **Create Calculated Field** button to bring up the **Add Field** dialog again. Notice how the calculation input box already has [Transaction Amount] pre-populated, as we can see in the following screenshot. That is the result of having the field selected when we clicked on **Create Calculated Field**:

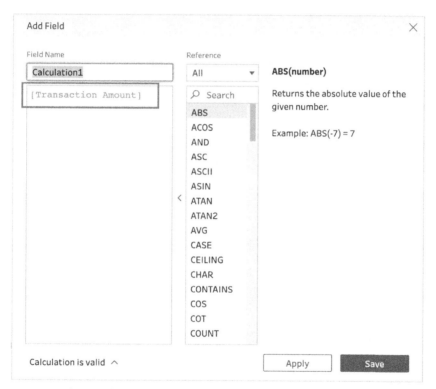

Figure 7.7 – The calculation input box already has [Transaction Amount] pre-populated

9.  In order to calculate the sales tax amount, we could create a calculation using only the **Subtotal** field included in the original source data. However, it is possible to use other calculated fields in a calculated field, meaning we can simply subtract `Subtotal` from our `Transaction Amount` calculated field in order to determine the amount of sales tax. To do this, update the calculation by adding `- [Subtotal]`, as shown in the following screenshot. You can either type in the entire calculation or leverage the autocomplete suggestions:

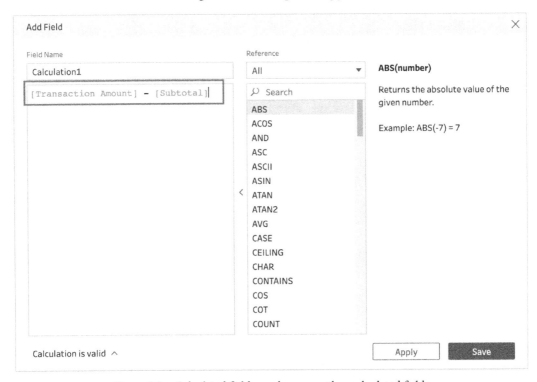

Figure 7.8 – Calculated fields can leverage other calculated fields

10. Name this field `Sales Tax Amount` and click **Save** to add it to your flow.

11. Re-arrange the newly added **Sales Tax Amount** field in your field list so that it is positioned after the **Subtotal** field:

Figure 7.9 – Drag the Sales Tax Amount field to reposition it

With these steps completed, you've successfully enriched your dataset by adding the **Sales Tax Amount** and **Transaction Amount** calculated fields.

## How it works...

In this recipe, we learned how to create calculated fields using basic arithmetic. We also learned that we could leverage existing calculated fields in a new calculation. We've seen that selecting a field prior to starting your calculation inserts that field into any new calculation. By typing in our calculation, we've seen Tableau Prep's autocomplete feature at work and you are now familiar with the functions section, which you can leverage anytime you need help finding or using a function. During this practice, we enriched our dataset and improved any downstream analysis processes that require the information we generated in the calculated fields. Preparing your data in this fashion can avoid many complications and speed up connected reports because they do not have to perform these calculations anymore. In general, applying calculated fields in your data preparation phase, rather than during the subsequent reporting phase, promotes data consistency for your organization.

# Creating conditional calculations

One of the most powerful calculations you can do is **conditional calculations**. Conditional calculations return a value based on the criteria you set in the calculation itself. When the conditions are met, a certain value is returned, as specified by you in the calculation. Because conditional statements are relatively resource-intensive on your computer's hardware, it is best to perform them during data preparation in **Tableau Prep** rather than a downstream analysis tool. By performing resource-intensive tasks in Tableau Prep, the data output will already contain the end result, preventing your analysis tools, such as **Tableau Desktop**, from having to perform these tasks at a less convenient time. In this recipe, we'll calculate the sales tax amount as well. However, this time, we're going to apply a different tax rate based on the department. To do so, we're going to use a conditional calculation.

## Getting ready

To follow along with this recipe, download the Sample Files 7.2 folder from this book's GitHub repository. There, you'll find the December 2016 Sales.xlsx Excel file we've used previously. The data contains sales data, including the subtotal amount due, excluding applicable taxes. In the previous recipe, we used a calculated field to determine the sales tax amount and total transaction amount by assuming a flat sales tax percentage set at 6.5%.

# How to do it...

Start by opening the December 2016 Sales.xlsx flow from the Sample Files 7.2 folder in **Tableau Prep**, then follow these steps:

1.  Add the **December 2016 Sales** sheet to your flow and connect a clean step, as shown in the following screenshot. Take note that our data includes the **Subtotal** amount, but not the sales tax amount or total transaction amount. Also note that the **Department** field contains three unique values. They are **Electronics**, **Groceries**, and **Household Appliances**:

Figure 7.10 – Add an input step and a clean step to get started

2.  Click on **Create Calculated Field** to bring up the **Add Field** dialog. Name the new calculation Sales Tax Amount:

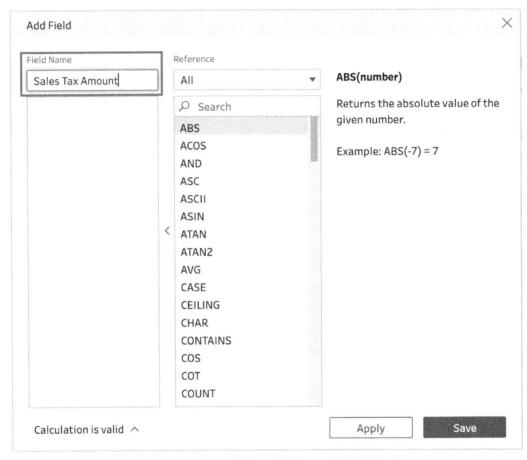

Figure 7.11 – Start a new calculated field named Sales Tax Amount

3.  Conditional calculations use logical functions. Filter the **Reference** list to **Logical**
    to see the available functions, then select **IF**. When you select a function, Tableau
    Prep will give you a brief outline of the functionality, as well as an example. Double-
    click **IF** so that it is added to your calculation input box, as shown in the following
    screenshot:

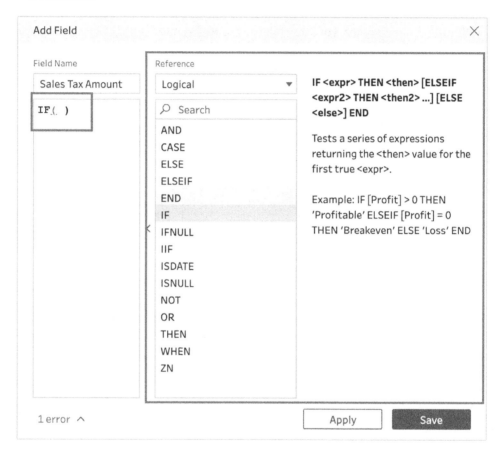

Figure 7.12 – Double-click IF in the function Reference list

4.  Let's write out our calculation and assume a tax rate of 21% for **Electronics**, 5% for **Groceries**, and 10% for **Household Appliances**. We'll start off with just **Electronics**. Remove the parentheses in the calculation and complete the calculation so that it reads IF [Department] = "Electronics" THEN [Subtotal] * 0.21 END. This calculation checks each row in your data and if **Department** is equal to **Electronics**, it will multiply the **Subtotal** amount by 0.21, or 21% (if you require additional screen space, you can collapse the **Reference** list by selecting the arrow in the middle of the screen):

Figure 7.13 – Complete the calculated field input

5.  You can see from the **Calculation is valid** text in the bottom-right corner of the calculation editor that this calculation is ready to be saved. Although it is incomplete for our purposes, the END keyword in our calculation indicates to Tableau Prep that this is the end of our IF expression. Save the calculation and observe the data preview values for the newly added **Sales Tax Amount** field:

| Sales Tax Amount | Date | Subtotal | Department | Cashier | Store ZIP | Store City | Store Region |
|---|---|---|---|---|---|---|---|
| 584.22 | 04/12/2016 | 2,782 | Electronics | Battle, Jane Q. | 31777 | Barrie | ON |
| null | 05/12/2016 | 3,943 | Groceries | Burch, Athena R. | B6X 4T1 | St. Petersburg | FL |
| 1,846.11 | 26/12/2016 | 8,791 | Electronics | Yates, Lewis O. | 27776 | Drachten | Fr |
| 1,691.97 | 16/12/2016 | 8,057 | Electronics | Farrell, Venus W. | 88825 | Ganganagar | RJ |
| null | 25/12/2016 | 2,665 | Groceries | Matthews, Stephen F. | 6895IZ | Alajuela | A |
| null | 21/12/2016 | 1,637 | Groceries | Barnes, Vaughan Y. | 42696 | Katsina | KT |
| null | 28/12/2016 | 2,947 | Groceries | Wooten, Scarlet J. | 34990 | Kawerau | North Island |
| null | 06/12/2016 | 6,522 | Household Appliances | Merrill, Suki G. | 37127 | Hamburg | Hamburg |
| null | 01/12/2016 | 1,665 | Groceries | Anthony, Joan C. | 71899 | Istanbul | Istanbul |
| null | 08/12/2016 | 5,945 | Household Appliances | Harmon, Remedios D. | 16153 | Merchtem | Vlaams-Brabant |
| null | 17/12/2016 | 3,757 | Household Appliances | Mccoy, Fritz L. | 42570 | LaSalle | Ontario |
| 717.99 | 18/12/2016 | 3,419 | Electronics | Landry, Yael Z. | 95578 | Aubagne | PR |
| 308.28 | 03/12/2016 | 1,468 | Electronics | Bush, Jennifer L. | N4R 8T3 | Cumberland | ON |

Figure 7.14 – Rows with a department other than Electronics contain null values for Sales Tax Amount

In our updated dataset, as shown in the previous screenshot, we can see that each row with a **Department** value of **Electronics** has the **Sales Tax Amount** field populated. However, all other rows, that is, those with **Groceries** or **Household Appliances**, have a **null** value for **Sales Tax Amount**. This exercise illustrates what happens when we do not provide what is known as a **catch-all**. A catch-all will allow us to set a value for any scenarios we have not anticipated, or at least not specified.

6.  Let's add a catch-all to our **Sales Tax Amount** calculated field. Expand the **Changes** pane and select the edit button for our calculated field to return to the calculation editor:

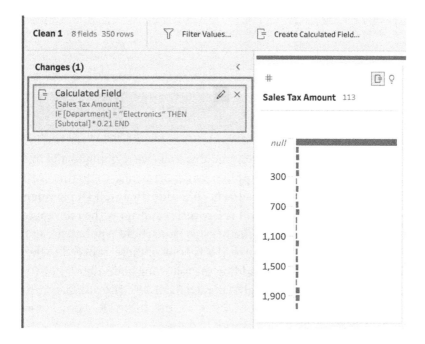

Figure 7.15 – You can view and edit calculated fields via the Changes pane

7.  Update the calculation by inserting ELSE  0 before END. This will tell Tableau Prep that if none of the conditions you specified are met, it should return a zero:

Figure 7.16 – Adding a catch-all to an IF function

8. Save the updated calculated field and observe the result in the data preview. All rows with **Groceries** or **Household Appliances** now have a **Sales Tax Amount** value set at zero:

| Sales Tax Amount | Date | Subtotal | Department | Cashier | Store ZIP | Store City | Store Region |
|---|---|---|---|---|---|---|---|
| 584.22 | 04/12/2016 | 2,782 | Electronics | Battle, Jane Q. | 31777 | Barrie | ON |
| 0 | 05/12/2016 | 3,943 | Groceries | Burch, Athena R. | B6X 4T1 | St. Petersburg | FL |
| 1,846.11 | 26/12/2016 | 8,791 | Electronics | Yates, Lewis O. | 27776 | Drachten | Fr |
| 1,691.97 | 16/12/2016 | 8,057 | Electronics | Farrell, Venus W. | 88825 | Ganganagar | RJ |
| 0 | 25/12/2016 | 2,665 | Groceries | Matthews, Stephen F. | 6895IZ | Alajuela | A |
| 0 | 21/12/2016 | 1,637 | Groceries | Barnes, Vaughan Y. | 42696 | Katsina | KT |
| 0 | 28/12/2016 | 2,947 | Groceries | Wooten, Scarlet J. | 34990 | Kawerau | North Island |
| 0 | 06/12/2016 | 6,522 | Household Appliances | Merrill, Suki G. | 37127 | Hamburg | Hamburg |
| 0 | 01/12/2016 | 1,665 | Groceries | Anthony, Joan C. | 71899 | Istanbul | Istanbul |
| 0 | 08/12/2016 | 5,945 | Household Appliances | Harmon, Remedios D. | 16153 | Merchtem | Vlaams-Brabant |
| 0 | 17/12/2016 | 3,757 | Household Appliances | Mccoy, Fritz L. | 42570 | LaSalle | Ontario |
| 717.99 | 18/12/2016 | 3,419 | Electronics | Landry, Yael Z. | 95578 | Aubagne | PR |
| 308.28 | 03/12/2016 | 1,468 | Electronics | Bush, Jennifer L. | N4R 8T3 | Cumberland | ON |

Figure 7.17 – Groceries and Household Appliances no longer have a null value for Sales Tax Amount

9. Head back to the calculation editor and this time, we're going to add in logic for the **Groceries** and **Household Appliances** departments. To do this, we'll use the `ELSEIF` statement after the current condition; that is, if **Department** is not **Electronics**, then check whether it is **Groceries** and apply the relevant tax rate, and if it's not **Groceries**, check whether it is **Household Appliances** and apply the relevant tax rate. And, of course, if it is none of these, proceed to the catch-all, zero. Update the calculation by adding the following code after `0.21` to evaluate the department and apply the right tax rate: `ELSEIF [Department] = "Groceries" THEN [Subtotal] * 0.05 ELSEIF [Department] = "Household Appliances" THEN [Subtotal] * 0.10`. You can move code onto new lines to make your calculation more legible. Save your calculation when ready:

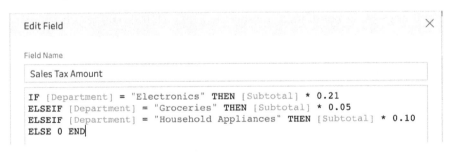

Figure 7.18 – Our final code

> **Important note**
>
> The calculation here can be written in different ways. We included some duplicative code here, namely [Subtotal] *. This is causing the calculation to become lengthier but easier to read. You may apply a different calculation, such as the following, to achieve the same output:
>
> ```
> [Subtotal]*
> IF [Department] = "Electronics" THEN 0.21
> ELSEIF [Department] = "Groceries" THEN 0.05
> ELSEIF [Department] = "Household Appliances" THEN
> 0.10
> ELSE 0 END
> ```

10. In the data preview, confirm that each **Department** type now has a calculated **Sales Tax Amount** value:

| Sales Tax Amount | Date | Subtotal | Department | Cashier | Store ZIP | Store City | Store Region |
|---|---|---|---|---|---|---|---|
| 584.22 | 04/12/2016 | 2,782 | Electronics | Battle, Jane Q. | 31777 | Barrie | ON |
| 197.15 | 05/12/2016 | 3,943 | Groceries | Burch, Athena R. | B6X 4T1 | St. Petersburg | FL |
| 1,846.11 | 26/12/2016 | 8,791 | Electronics | Yates, Lewis O. | 27776 | Drachten | Fr |
| 1,691.97 | 16/12/2016 | 8,057 | Electronics | Farrell, Venus W. | 88825 | Ganganagar | RJ |
| 133.25 | 25/12/2016 | 2,665 | Groceries | Matthews, Stephen F. | 6895IZ | Alajuela | A |
| 81.85 | 21/12/2016 | 1,637 | Groceries | Barnes, Vaughan Y. | 42696 | Katsina | KT |
| 147.35 | 28/12/2016 | 2,947 | Groceries | Wooten, Scarlet J. | 34990 | Kawerau | North Island |
| 652.2 | 06/12/2016 | 6,522 | Household Appliances | Merrill, Suki G. | 37127 | Hamburg | Hamburg |
| 83.25 | 01/12/2016 | 1,665 | Groceries | Anthony, Joan C. | 71899 | Istanbul | Istanbul |
| 594.5 | 08/12/2016 | 5,945 | Household Appliances | Harmon, Remedios D. | 16153 | Merchtem | Vlaams-Brabant |
| 375.70000000000005 | 17/12/2016 | 3,757 | Household Appliances | Mccoy, Fritz L. | 42570 | LaSalle | Ontario |
| 717.99 | 18/12/2016 | 3,419 | Electronics | Landry, Yael Z. | 95578 | Aubagne | PR |
| 308.28 | 03/12/2016 | 1,468 | Electronics | Bush, Jennifer L. | N4R 8T3 | Cumberland | ON |

Figure 7.19 – Confirm each Department type has a Sales Tax Amount value

With these steps completed, you've successfully added a conditional calculation and determined the **sales tax amount** based on the **department**.

## How it works...

In this recipe, we learned how to apply conditional calculations using Tableau Prep's logical functions. We learned that we could use conditions to perform a given calculation. Conditions are one of the most powerful calculation functions you can employ in order to prepare your data and account for various scenarios, as we've done with the **Department** field in this recipe. By using calculated fields, we were able to determine a new value, **Sales Tax Amount**, based on the value of another field, **Department**. Conditional calculations are evaluated row by row and may be resource-intensive, which will be noticeable when working with relatively large datasets and running your flow. Nonetheless, applying these powerful calculations during data preparation will benefit downstream analysis since the output of Tableau Prep will already include the calculated value.

# Extracting substrings

More often than not, data is delivered to us in a less-than-ideal state, with multiple values being held in a single field. We saw how to split data into multiple fields in the *Splitting columns with multiple values* recipe, in *Chapter 3, Cleaning Transformations*. However, splitting fields relies on the data being organized, and will never leave out any of the data. In this recipe, we'll look at extracting substrings, which will result in new fields as well. However, unlike splitting fields, we'll be able to more narrowly define what data we want to include in our new field. Furthermore, extracting substrings is non-destructive, that is, the original field will remain unaffected. In this recipe, we'll load a dataset into Tableau Prep that has a field with multiple values in it. We'll then proceed to extract each value and create separate fields for each.

## Getting ready

To follow along with this recipe, download the `Sample Files 7.3` folder from this book's GitHub repository. There, you'll find the `December 2016 Sales.xlsx` Excel file. In the version of the sales data we've been using throughout this book, you'll find that we have a field called `Customer Name`. The `Customer Name` field holds multiple values: the name of the customer, organized by last name, first name, middle name, and initial.

# How to do it...

Start by opening the December 2016 Sales.xlsx flow from the Sample Files 7.3 folder in **Tableau Prep**, then follow these steps:

1.  Add a clean step to your flow and examine your data in the data preview grid. Observe the **Customer Name** field to confirm its contents are organized by last name, first name, middle name, and initial:

| Date | Transaction Amount | Department | Customer Name | Store ZIP | Store City | Store Region |
|------|-------------------|------------|---------------|-----------|------------|--------------|
| 04/12/2016 | 2,782 | Electronics | Battle, Jane Q. | 31777 | Barrie | ON |
| 05/12/2016 | 3,943 | Groceries | Burch, Athena R. | B6X 4T1 | St. Petersburg | FL |
| 26/12/2016 | 8,791 | Electronics | Yates, Lewis O. | 27776 | Drachten | Fr |
| 16/12/2016 | 8,057 | Electronics | Farrell, Venus W. | 88825 | Ganganagar | RJ |
| 25/12/2016 | 2,665 | Groceries | Matthews, Stephen F. | 68951Z | Alajuela | A |
| 21/12/2016 | 1,637 | Groceries | Barnes, Vaughan Y. | 42696 | Katsina | KT |
| 28/12/2016 | 2,947 | Groceries | Wooten, Scarlet J. | 34990 | Kawerau | North Island |

Figure 7.20 – Verify the organization of the Customer Name field

2.  Let's first extract the last name substring. Click on **Create Calculated Field** and name your new calculation Last Name.

3.  Since the last name is always followed by a comma, we are going to locate the position of the comma first. To do this, enter the `FIND([Customer Name],",")` calculation. The `FIND` function will evaluate a given field, **Customer Name** in this case, and locate a given substring, a *comma* character in our use case. When the `FIND` function locates the *comma* substring, it will return its position number:

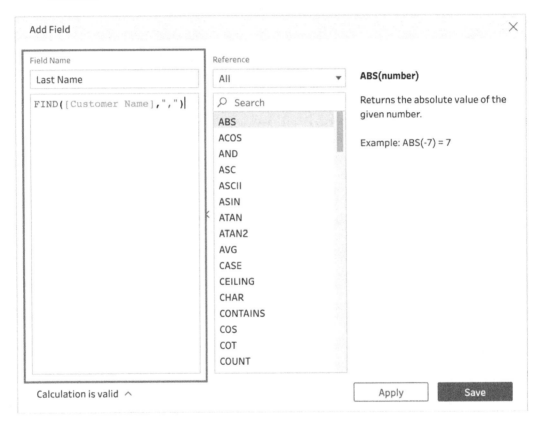

Figure 7.21 – Use the FIND function to locate a substring position

4. Click **Save** to add your new calculated field to the dataset and observe the results. The number indicates the position of the comma character in the **Customer Name** field. For example, the name **Yates, Lewis O.** has a comma character located at position 6. The first five characters make up the name **Yates**, and the sixth character is the comma:

| Last Name | Date | Transaction Amount | Department | Customer Name | Store ZIP | Store City | Store Region |
|---|---|---|---|---|---|---|---|
| 7 | 04/12/2016 | 2,782 | Electronics | Battle, Jane Q. | 31777 | Barrie | ON |
| 6 | 05/12/2016 | 3,943 | Groceries | Burch, Athena R. | B6X 4T1 | St. Petersburg | FL |
| 6 | 26/12/2016 | 8,791 | Electronics | Yates, Lewis O. | 27776 | Drachten | Fr |
| 8 | 16/12/2016 | 8,057 | Electronics | Farrell, Venus W. | 88825 | Ganganagar | RJ |
| 9 | 25/12/2016 | 2,665 | Groceries | Matthews, Stephen F. | 6895IZ | Alajuela | A |
| 7 | 21/12/2016 | 1,637 | Groceries | Barnes, Vaughan Y. | 42696 | Katsina | KT |
| 7 | 28/12/2016 | 2,947 | Groceries | Wooten, Scarlet J. | 34990 | Kawerau | North Island |

Figure 7.22 – Verify the result of your calculation in the preview pane

5. We need to amend our calculation in order to return the last name in full. To amend an existing calculation, expand the **Changes** pane, then click on the edit icon for our calculated field, as highlighted in the following screenshot:

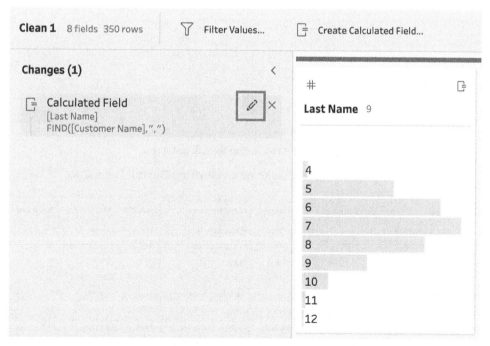

Figure 7.23 – Open up the Changes pane in order to locate the edit button for calculated fields

6.  We want to get all the starting characters of the string, up to the comma character position, excluding the comma. To do this, we can use the LEFT function. LEFT will return a specified number of characters from a given string. Update your calculation to LEFT([Customer Name],FIND([Customer Name],",")-1). Here, we're instructing the LEFT function to get a substring from the **Customer Name** field, specifically the first number of characters as defined by the FIND function we wrote in *Step 3*. Notice how we added -1 to the FIND function, in order to exclude the comma character itself:

Figure 7.24 – Extracting the full last name

7.  Verify, in the data preview, that we're now returning the full last name:

| Last Name | Date | Transaction Amount | Department | Customer Name | Store ZIP | Store City | Store Region |
|---|---|---|---|---|---|---|---|
| Battle | 04/12/2016 | 2,782 | Electronics | Battle, Jane Q. | 31777 | Barrie | ON |
| Burch | 05/12/2016 | 3,943 | Groceries | Burch, Athena R. | B6X 4T1 | St. Petersburg | FL |
| Yates | 26/12/2016 | 8,791 | Electronics | Yates, Lewis O. | 27776 | Drachten | Fr |
| Farrell | 16/12/2016 | 8,057 | Electronics | Farrell, Venus W. | 88825 | Ganganagar | RJ |
| Matthews | 25/12/2016 | 2,665 | Groceries | Matthews, Stephen F. | 68951Z | Alajuela | A |
| Barnes | 21/12/2016 | 1,637 | Groceries | Barnes, Vaughan Y. | 42696 | Katsina | KT |
| Wooten | 28/12/2016 | 2,947 | Groceries | Wooten, Scarlet J. | 34990 | Kawerau | North Island |

Figure 7.25 – The last name is now an individual field in your dataset

8.  Next, we are going to return the first name. Click on **Create Calculated Field** and name your new field `First Name`. Enter the `SPLIT([Customer Name]," ",2)` calculation. In this calculation, we're using the `SPLIT` function to separate values in the **Customer Name** column by a given character. The character we've specified between the quotation marks is blank, so we're splitting by an empty space. In doing so, we get three parts in our **Customer Name** field, that is, **last name**, **first name**, and **middle initial**. Since we want the second part, we specify 2 in the `SPLIT` function. Click **Save** to add your new field.

9.  Next, let's create our final field for the middle initial. Click **Create Calculated Field** and name it `Middle Initial`. Enter the `RIGHT([Customer Name],2)` calculation. This calculation uses the `RIGHT` function. `RIGHT` will return the number of specified, in this case, 2, rightmost characters in the **Customer Name** field. Click **Save** to add your new field.

10. To organize your dataset, drag the **Middle Initial** field between the **First Name** and **Last Name** fields.

11. We do not need the **Customer Name** field anymore. We can safely remove it and the three derived calculations will continue to function. Go ahead and remove the **Customer Name** field from your flow:

Figure 7.26 – Our final, refined dataset

With these steps completed, you've successfully transformed your dataset by extracting three different substrings from the original **Customer Name** field.

## How it works...

In this recipe, we learned how to create calculated fields using various string functions: LEFT, RIGHT, SPLIT, and FIND. Using each of these functions, we extracted a specific part of a text string, using LEFT or RIGHT to get the beginning or ending characters, SPLIT to break up a field into separate values, and FIND to locate the position of a substring so that we may then extract it. These are powerful functions as they allow you to create dynamic data extraction from a field. For example, the comma character we located using the FIND function could be in a different position in every row or every time the dataset is refreshed. Using this function, Tableau Prep will always evaluate the field to locate the right position first.

# Changing date formats with calculations

When you work with many different disparate systems, you're bound to run into a scenario where a date is formatted in such a way that it isn't recognized by Tableau Prep as a date. As a result, Tableau Prep will set the data type for such a field to a string. So, we don't lose any data, but we cannot perform any date functions on such a field. To resolve this, we can create a calculation to re-organize the date string so that the newly added field can be recognized as a date. In this recipe, we'll process a data file using Tableau Prep that holds a date field with values not recognized as a date by Tableau. During the process, we'll change the format of the field using a calculation so that Tableau will then correctly recognize the field as a date data type.

## Getting ready

To follow along with this recipe, download the Sample Files 7.4 folder from this book's GitHub repository. There, you'll find the December 2016 Sales.csv Excel file.

# How to do it...

Start by connecting to the December 2016 Sales.csv file from the Sample Files 7.4 folder in **Tableau Prep**, then follow these steps:

1.  Before adding any additional tools, observe the **Date** field and its data type in the input step. Note that **Type** did not auto-detect a date and the sample values appear formatted as numbers:

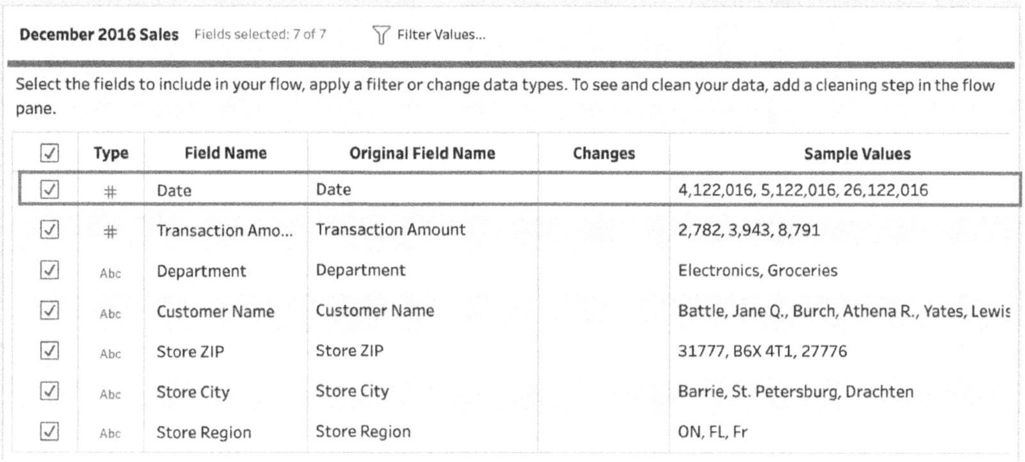

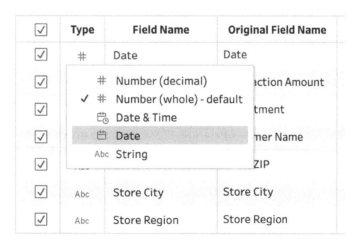

Figure 7.27 – Evaluate your input step data

2.  Click the # symbol in the **Type** column and set the data type to **String**:

Figure 7.28 – Change the Date data type to String

> **Important note**
>
> You can change the data type of any field during an input step, or in any subsequent clean step. However, in this particular scenario, we'll want to change the data type during the input step. The reason for this is that Tableau Prep has detected the field as a number, and if we pass data along to the next step with this setting, we'll lose the leading zero some dates have. For example, December 4, 2016 exists in our source file as `04122016`. Setting the format to string during the input step retains the leading zero and makes our subsequent calculations easier.

3.  Add a clean step and determine the date format by reviewing the data in the preview pane. It seems our data is formatted as `DDMMYYYY`, that is, two digits to indicate the day, two digits to indicate the month, and four to indicate the year, without any separator symbols:

| Date | Transaction Amount | Department | Customer Name | Store ZIP | Store City | Store Region |
|------|--------------------|------------|---------------|-----------|------------|--------------|
| 04122016 | 2,782 | Electronics | Battle, Jane Q. | 31777 | Barrie | ON |
| 05122016 | 3,943 | Groceries | Burch, Athena R. | B6X 4T1 | St. Petersburg | FL |
| 26122016 | 8,791 | Electronics | Yates, Lewis O. | 27776 | Drachten | Fr |
| 16122016 | 8,057 | Electronics | Farrell, Venus W. | 88825 | Ganganagar | RJ |
| 25122016 | 2,665 | Groceries | Matthews, Stephe | 6895IZ | Alajuela | A |
| 21122016 | 1,637 | Groceries | Barnes, Vaughan Y | 42696 | Katsina | KT |
| 28122016 | 2,947 | Groceries | Wooten, Scarlet J. | 34990 | Kawerau | North Island |

Figure 7.29 – Evaluate your data in order to determine the date format

4.  Click on **Create Calculated Field** and name your new field `Date`.

> **Important note**
>
> We already have a field name of **Date** in our dataset. When you name any new calculated field the same as an existing field in your dataset, Tableau Prep will automatically hide the original field and show the calculated field instead. This is a great feature to speed up your flow design as we do not have to manually remove the soon-to-be-redundant source **Date** field.

5.  Enter the MID([Date],3,2) + "-" + LEFT([Date],2) + "-" +
    RIGHT([Date],4) calculation. We've seen the LEFT and RIGHT functions in
    action in previous recipes. The **MID** function is one we have not used before. MID
    returns a substring from a given field, starting at a certain position. In this case, MID
    takes the **Date** field, starts at the third character, and returns the subsequent two
    characters. In doing so, it returns our month value. Because our source field has
    a string data type, we can apply string functions, which we've done by adding text in
    the form of + "-" +. In string fields, the plus symbol concatenates values, rather
    than adding them:

Figure 7.30 – Calculate a correct date format

> **Important note**
>
> As we saw in *Step 3*, the date format in our source is day, month, year. Yet in
> our calculation, we organized it as month, day, year. The reason for this
> US-style date formatting is that is the format that Tableau Prep will recognize,
> as we'll see in *Step 6*.

6.  Click **Save** to view your calculation result. Notice how the newly added **Date** calculation has replaced the source **Date** field. It now looks like a date. However, the type is still **String**. Click the type icon for the **Date** field and change it to **Date**:

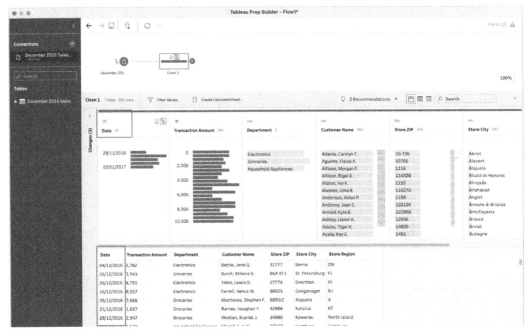

Figure 7.31 – Change the type format to Date

With these steps completed, you have successfully transformed your data into a proper date format.

## How it works...

In this recipe, we learned how to leverage calculations to change a string field to a date. We did so by breaking down the values in our dataset, specifically identifying and extracting the day, month, and year values. We then re-arranged these values and formatted them with additional symbols to create the appearance of a properly formatted date. We then changed the data type to **Date** and in doing so, added benefits to any further calculations you may wish to perform that involve date functions, either in Tableau Prep or an analytics application such as Tableau Desktop.

# Creating relative temporal calculations

There are many analytics scenarios where you may want to calculate a date-related field based on a relative date, such as today or this year. Such calculations can make your Tableau Prep flow more dynamic and each time the flow is run, Tableau Prep will evaluate the data against the current date or time period. In this recipe, we'll perform a calculation using today's date as a relative anchor. That is, if you execute the flow on July 4, our calculation will use July 4 as a relative point in time. If you execute the same flow the next day, Tableau Prep will automatically adjust to July 5. In this recipe, we'll calculate the age of support tickets for a company's helpdesk, relative to today, that is, how long a support ticket has been open.

## Getting ready

To follow along with this recipe, download the `Sample Files 7.5` folder from this book's GitHub repository. There, you'll find the `Support Requests Extract.csv` Excel file. In this file, we find an extract from a company's helpdesk, listing their support tickets, including the date a ticket was submitted by a customer.

## How to do it...

Start by opening the `Support Requests Extract.csv` flow from the `Sample Files 7.5` folder in **Tableau Prep**, then follow these steps:

1. Add a clean step and examine the data. Note that the data includes a field named **DateSubmitted**, which represents the date a customer logged a support request. We can also see the status of these requests in the **Status** field. The **Status** field shows us three distinct states: **New**, **In Progress**, and **Resolved**:

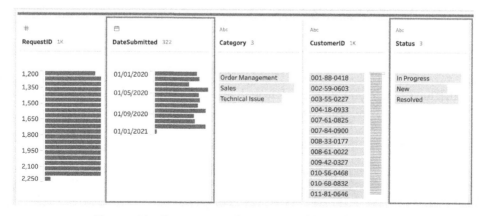

Figure 7.32 – Examine your data prior to adding calculations

2.  Suppose we want to calculate the age for each open request relative to the current date, that is, requests with a status of either *New* or *In Progress*. To do this, click on **Create Calculated Field** and name your new field Age.

> **Important note**
> Data preparation for downstream analytics can significantly speed up your analytics flow. However, caution is advised when working with relative dates. For example, in the calculation we're about to perform, we'll calculate a value relative to the current date, that is, the date that you execute your flow. If you have a scenario with downstream reports that are dependent on your Tableau Prep flow output, you may want to ensure the flow runs every day, such that the outcome of the calculation is always updated, relative to the current date.

3.  To calculate the number of days between the date a support request was submitted and the current date, enter the following calculation: DATEDIFF('day',[DateSubmitted],TODAY()). The DATEDIFF function we use here calculates the difference between two dates. First, we specify the date part as day. This is the granularity of the date difference. For example, we could have set this to month in order to get the difference in months rather than days. Then, we specify the start date, in this case, the DateSubmitted field, and the end date, which is our relative date. The current date is returned by the TODAY() function:

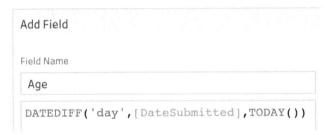

Figure 7.33 – Use the TODAY relative date function

4.  Click **Save** to add your newly calculated field and view the **Age** field containing the number of days since the support request was opened, relative to the current date.

5.  Open up the **Changes** pane and select the edit icon to edit your **Age** field. We're going to amend the calculation to calculate the age only for those requests with a status of **New** or **In Progress**. To do so, we'll use the conditional `IF` function. Modify your calculation to `IF [Status]!="Resolved"THEN DATEDIFF('day',[DateSubmitted],TODAY()) ELSE NULL END`. Here, we're telling Tableau Prep to perform our age calculation only if **Status** is not equal to **Resolved**. We indicate the not-equal-to operator as `!=`. If the status is anything else, it'll simply return `null`:

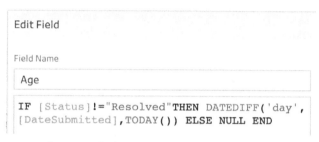

Figure 7.34 – Make your calculation conditional, based on the Status field value

6.  Click **Save** to apply your calculation changes and confirm that the values in the data preview pane show **null** for those rows where **Status** is **Resolved**.

Having completed these steps, you've successfully added a relative temporal calculation.

## How it works...

In this recipe, we learned how to leverage the TODAY relative function in order to perform a calculation using the current date as a reference point in time. The TODAY function will always update relative to the present day. That is, if today is January 1, 2021, the calculation will replace TODAY with January 1, 2021. However, if you run that same flow on January 2, 2021, then Tableau Prep will automatically replace TODAY with January 2, 2021. Another relative function in Tableau Prep is the NOW function, which will return the current date and time, rather than the date alone. Using these functions can make your flow more dynamic.

# Creating regular expressions in calculations

In this chapter, we've seen how to extract substrings already. In this brief recipe, we're going to explore another method of doing so, using regular expressions. Regular expressions, also referred to as regex, allow you to define a complex search pattern to locate, and in our case extract, substrings. A look at the inner workings of regex is beyond the scope of this book, but a quick web search will reveal numerous sources including example regex statements. In Tableau Prep, you can leverage such statements in a REGEX function.

## Getting ready

To follow along with this recipe, download the Sample Files 7.6 folder from this book's GitHub repository. There, you'll find the Missed Chats.csv Excel file. In this file, we find a log of users who have visited our company website and attempted to contact us via live chat when no agent was available to respond. At that point, they submitted their details in a contact form so that our agents can contact those users at a later date. However, the data produced by the form is not organized, and the customer name, company name, email, and address are all combined in one single field.

## How to do it...

Start by opening the Missed Chats.csv flow from the Sample Files 7.6 folder in **Tableau Prep**, then follow these steps:

1.  Add a clean step and examine the data. Suppose we are interested in the email address only, which is contained in the long string in the **Customer Info** field. We could perform some nifty detective work with functions such as LEFT, RIGHT, MIDDLE, and FIND in order to locate the email. Alternatively, we can provide a single regex statement to extract the email, which is what we'll do in this recipe:

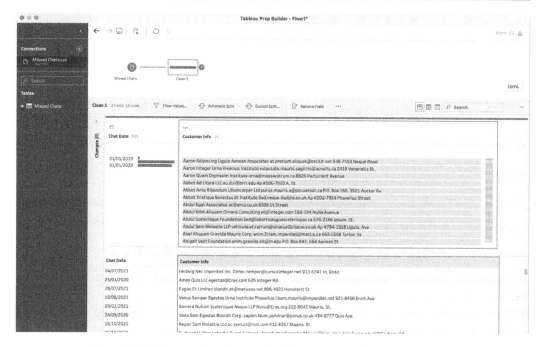

Figure 7.35 – Observe how the email address is captured in the source date

2.  Click on **Create Calculated Field** and name it Email. Tableau Prep can return the result of a regular expression using the REGEXP_EXTRACT function. It can simply return true or false if a substring is located by regex, using the REGEXP_MATCH function. It can also replace the value found by regex, using the REGEXP_REPLACE function. Since we want to extract the email itself, we'll use REGEXP_EXTRACT. Type in the REGEXP_EXTRACT([Customer Info],'...') calculation. This is the basis for the function. You can replace the three dots with any valid regex expression. Replace it with the following expression, designed to locate an email address: ([a-zA-Z0-9._-]+@[a-zA-Z0-9._-]+\.[a-zA-Z0-9_-]+):

Figure 7.36 – Use REGEXP_EXTRACT to extract the string located by a regular expression

3.  Click **Save** to add your newly calculated **Email** field and validate the email addresses extracted:

| Email | Chat Date | Customer Info |
|---|---|---|
| et@Donec.ca | 07/02/2021 | Deirdre Ullamcorper Magna Foundation et@Donec.ca 4 |
| vitae.dolor.Donec@diamSed.ca | 02/01/2021 | Mason Mi Associates vitae.dolor.Donec@diamSed.ca P. |
| ornare.placerat.orci@nisiaodio.edu | 12/03/2021 | Colby Nulla Ante Foundation ornare.placerat.orci@nisi |
| faucibus.Morbi.vehicula@tincidunt.net | 26/02/2021 | Joy Tristique Senectus Et Ltd faucibus.Morbi.vehicula@ |
| ante.Nunc@Maurismolestiepharetra.net | 23/09/2020 | Maisie Pellentesque Habitant LLP ante.Nunc@Maurism |
| vulputate.mauris.sagittis@acnulla.ca | 24/02/2021 | Aaron Integer Urna Vivamus Institute vulputate.mauri: |
| gravida.Aliquam.tincidunt@utipsumac.net | 03/08/2020 | Uma Odio Vel PC gravida.Aliquam.tincidunt@utipsuma |

Figure 7.37 – The newly added field contains the email addresses

With these simple steps completed, you've successfully applied regular expression string extraction.

## How it works...

In this recipe, we learned how to apply a regular expression in a Tableau Prep calculation. In our example, the regular expression we used searched for a given pattern that represents an email address, that is, a number of characters, followed by the @ symbol, followed by another string of characters, a full stop ( . ), and another string of characters. Regular expressions are an incredibly powerful text search function used by many different tools, including Tableau Prep. When basic string functions, such as LEFT, RIGHT, and FIND, are insufficient, regular expressions can be employed to execute a complex search pattern.

# 8
# Data Science in Tableau Prep Builder

In this chapter, you'll learn how to go beyond the built-in capabilities in Tableau Prep Builder by extending it with R and Python code. R and Python are two of the world's most popular programming languages and can perform numerous data science functions. Tableau Prep allows you to pass your data to an R or Python script at any stage during your flow, with the exception of the input data step. When you insert a script, Tableau Prep will pass the data to R or Python using an API. The script will execute in the R or Python environment and then output the results back to Tableau Prep and your flow continues. The ability to embed scripts allows you to greatly improve the functionality of Tableau Prep and perform advanced functions that are not otherwise possible.

In this chapter, we're going to cover the following main topics:

- Preparing Tableau Prep to work with R
- Embedding R code in a Tableau Prep flow
- Forecasting time series using R
- Preparing Tableau Prep to work with Python
- Embedding Python code in a Tableau Prep flow

# Technical requirements

To follow along with the recipes in this chapter, you will need **Tableau Prep Builder**, an internet connection, and administrative rights to install software.

The recipes in this chapter use sample data files that you can download from the book's GitHub repository: `https://github.com/PacktPublishing/Tableau-Prep-Cookbook`.

# Preparing Tableau Prep to work with R

R is a statistical programming language favored by many data scientists. It is available free of charge and benefits from a vast online community for ideation and support. To find out more about R, visit `https://www.r-project.org/about.html`. R by itself does not support interaction with other applications such as Tableau Prep. In order to extend R with that functionality, we need to install **Rserve** in addition to R itself.

> **Important note**
>
> The R programming language and the R and RStudio application interfaces are not part of Tableau Prep; they are separate technologies. An in-depth look at R is beyond the scope of this book. However, every system is slightly different, and you may run into unexpected challenges. For help, please refer to the R website: `https://cran.r-project.org`.

In this recipe, we will provide general guidance for configuring your system successfully.

## Getting ready

To follow along with this recipe, download the `Sample Files 8.1` folder from this book's GitHub repository.

# How to do it...

Start by opening your browser, then follow these steps to configure your machine:

1. Browse to `https://cran.r-project.org/mirrors.html`. Select any of the sites listed, nearest to your physical location. For example, in the **US**, you may select `https://mirror.las.iastate.edu/CRAN/`:

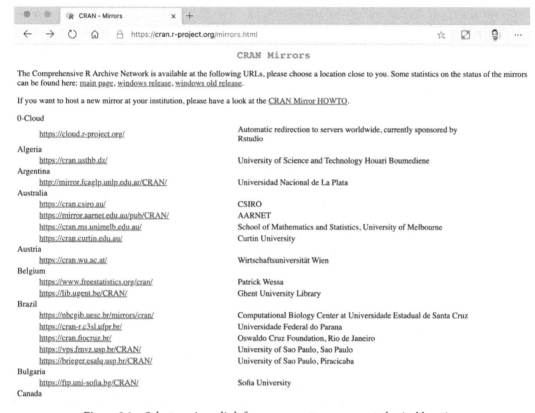

Figure 8.1 – Select a mirror link for your country or nearest physical location

2. Select the download link for your operating system at the top of the page in the **Precompiled binary distributions** section:

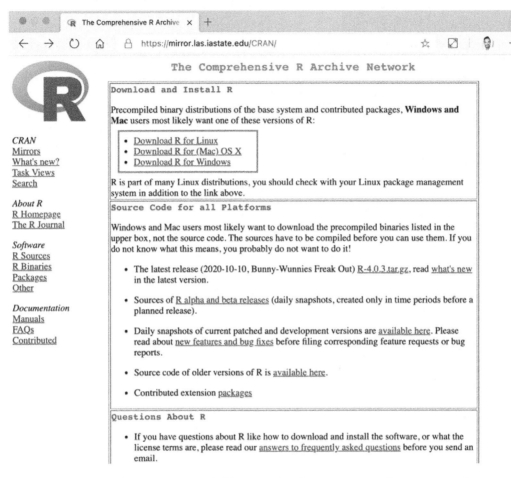

Figure 8.2 – Selecting a precompiled binary makes for an easier installation process than using the source code

3. If you're on a **Mac**, select the latest .PKG file, which indicates **notarized and signed** to commence the download. If you've selected **Windows**, select **base**, then click the **download** link.

4. Open up the downloaded installer and proceed through the installation, accepting all the default settings:

Figure 8.3 – Install R using all the default settings

5.  In addition to **R** itself, we are going to install **RStudio Desktop**. RStudio is an **IDE** for R. An IDE gives you an interface that allows you to interact with R a little easier. Browse to `https://rstudio.com/products/rstudio/download/` and select the installer for your operating system in order to commence the download:

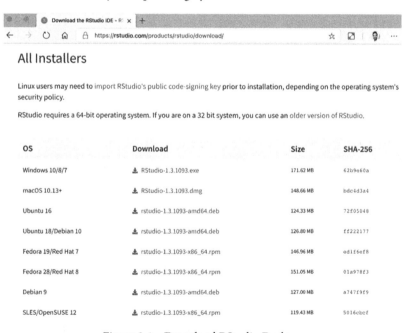

Figure 8.4 – Download RStudio Desktop

6.  When the download has completed, install RStudio Desktop. Accept any default options during the installation process.

7. Next, we need to download the **Rserve** package. Rserve is a package that allows Tableau Prep to communicate with R. Go to `https://www.rforge.net/Rserve/files/` and download the most recent snapshot.

> **Important note**
>
> Depending on your system configuration, not all versions may work for you. At the time of writing, we found that version 1.8.7 works for our intended purposes on both macOS and Windows. If you are familiar with RStudio, note that we are downloading the latest snapshot manually rather than using the built-in package manager, as the package manager may install an earlier version that has compatibility challenges.

The following screenshot shows the **Rserve** download page on the **RForge** website:

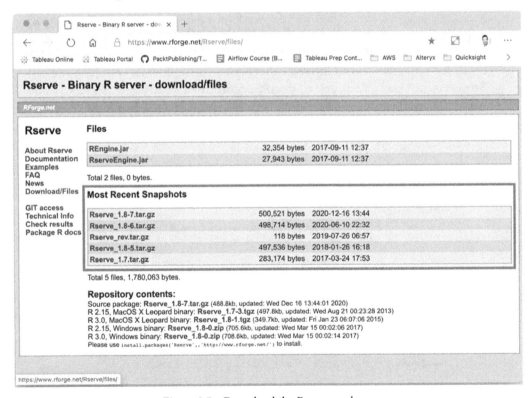

Figure 8.5 – Download the Rserve package

8. Launch the **RStudio** application. From the toolbar, select **Tools** then **Install Packages** to bring up the package installer dialog. There, set the **Install from** dropdown to **Package Archive File (.zip; .tar.gz)**. Doing so will bring up a file selector dialog where you can select the Rserve package file you just downloaded in *Step 7*:

Figure 8.6 – Install the Rserve package

9.  Click the **Install** button to install the Rserve package. The **Console** tab in RStudio will give you installation notes as it installs the package, which may take a few minutes. When the console displays **DONE (Rserve)**, the installation has completed. You can also confirm the package is installed by searching for `rserve` in the **Packages** tab at the bottom right:

Figure 8.7 – Confirm package installation by searching for rserve

10. Next, we need to start up Rserve, which will allow Tableau Prep to talk to R. To do this, enter the `library(Rserve)` command in the RStudio console and press the *Return* key. This will give the command line access to the Rserve package. Then, run the `Rserve(args=" --no-save --RS-conf ~/Documents/Rserv.cfg")` command to start up Rserve. The console will state `Rserv started in daemon mode` once Rserve is running:

Figure 8.8 – Finalize the R setup by starting Rserve

> **Important note**
>
> If you ever need to start Rserve again, for example, after your computer reboots, simply issue these two commands again.

11. Now that Rserve is running, we need to tell Tableau Prep how to connect to it. To do this, open up Tableau Prep and from the **Help** menu, select **Settings and Performance**, followed by **Manage Analytics Extension Connection**:

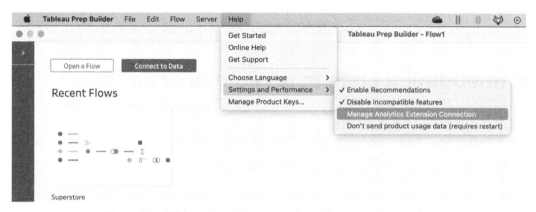

Figure 8.9 – Tableau Prep Manage Analytics Extension Connection

12. Select **Rserve** from the dropdown, then set the server to **localhost** and the port to **6311**, which are the defaults. Since we're using defaults, there is no username or password to set and so we can leave these fields blank. Click **Sign In** to complete the connection setup. Note that Tableau Prep will simply close the dialog without giving you a saved confirmation:

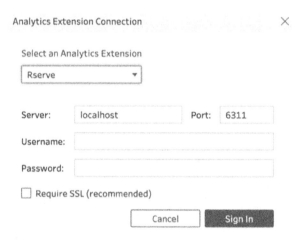

Figure 8.10 – Set up your connection to Rserve

This completes setting up R, Rserve, and Tableau Prep to talk to each other. From now on, you can start leveraging R scripts in your flows. In the next recipe, *Embedding R code in a Tableau Prep flow*, we'll do exactly that.

## How it works...

In this recipe, we learned how to configure your Mac or Windows PC with R, RStudio, and Rserve. This will allow Tableau Prep to pass data to R for R to run a script against that data and return the results to Tableau Prep. Since R is a programming language, you can write virtually any function you desire, greatly expanding the functionality of Tableau Prep.

# Embedding R code in a Tableau Prep flow

In the previous recipe, you learned how to configure your machine with R. You also set up a connection from Tableau Prep to R, using the Rserve package. In this recipe, we'll leverage that foundational setup to run an R script using Tableau Prep. We'll learn how to embed a script in our flow and understand how R sends the data back to our Tableau Prep data flow. The examples used are simple but form a solid foundation. Once you have mastered the basics, you'll be able to implement more advanced scripts, such as the script in the recipe titled *Forecasting time series using R*.

## Getting ready

To follow along with this recipe, download the `Sample Files 8.2` folder from this book's GitHub repository.

> **Important note**
> R is a programming language of its own, not covered by this book. We'll look at R code in this recipe at a very high level only, so you will gain sufficient knowledge to integrate R with Tableau Prep. However, a look at the R language itself is beyond the scope of this book.

## How to do it...

Start by opening up Tableau Prep and connecting to the `Transaction Amount by Date.xlsx` Excel file included in the sample files for this recipe, then follow these steps:

1.  Click the + icon on the input step, then select **Script** to add an analytic script step:

Analytics Extension Connection                                    ✕

Select an Analytics Extension

Rserve                                    ▾

Server:    localhost                    Port:    6311

Username:

Password:

☐ Require SSL (recommended)

Cancel        **Sign In**

Figure 8.11 – Adding an analytic script step

2.  At the time of writing, Tableau Prep supports **R** and **Python** scripts. Both use the same **analytic script step**, and so we'll need to indicate which language we're using here. Since **Rserve** is the default, we can leave the setting as is. To complete the step configuration, we need to select an R script file and set the function name. Included in the sample files for this recipe is a file named `R_functions_for_Tableau.R`. For the moment, leave Tableau Prep and open the file in a text editor such as **TextEdit**, **Notepad**, or **Sublime**:

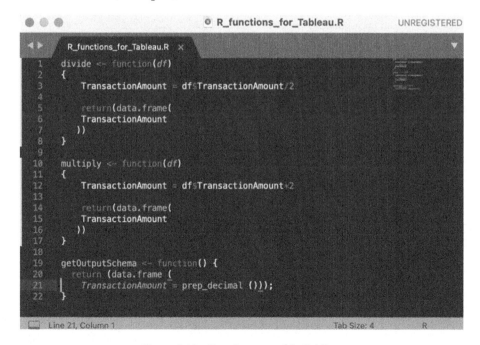

Figure 8.12 – R script opened in Sublime

This sample script contains three functions that'll help you better understand how to use R and Tableau Prep together.

The first eight lines contain a function named `divide`. The function uses the data from a DataFrame, `df`. Whenever you write an R script for Tableau Prep, calling a function with `(df)` will result in Tableau Prep passing data to that function.

This example function does nothing more than dividing a given number by 2.

Lines 10 to 17 demonstrate a similar function, `multiply`. Again, we see the use of `(df)` to pass data from Tableau Prep to this function. The function itself multiplies a given number by 2.

Lines 19 to 22 include a function named `getOutputSchema`. Whenever you want R to return data to Tableau Prep, you must use this function to do so. In this example, we're returning the `TransactionAmount` field to Tableau Prep. In this function, in addition to the name of the field to return, we must specify the data type for Tableau Prep. In this example, you can see that the data type for `TransactionAmount` has been set to `prep_string()`, which tells Tableau Prep that this field has a `string` data type.

The following table lists the various data types that are available, along with their respective functions to use in R:

| Data Type | R Function |
| --- | --- |
| String | prep_string() |
| Decimal | prep_decimal() |
| Integer | prep_int() |
| Boolean | prep_bool() |
| Date | prep_date() |
| DateTime | prep_datetime() |

3. Return to Tableau Prep and in the **Script** step, click **Browse** to select the `R_functions_for_Tableau.R` script from the sample files folder. Then, set the function name to `divide` and press the *Return* key:

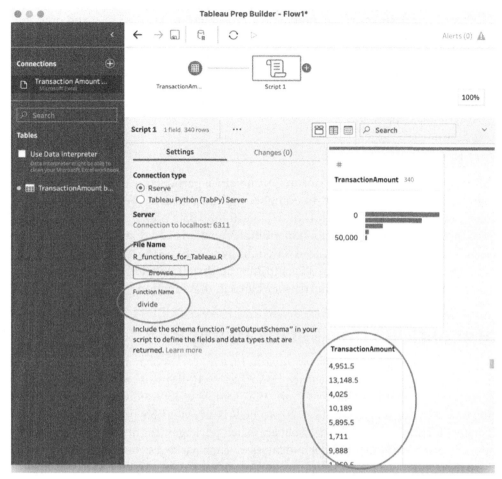

Figure 8.13 – Complete configuring the Script step

Pressing the *Return* key will instantly run the data through the R script. If successful, you will see the **TransactionAmount** field returned in Tableau Prep, with its original values divided by 2.

---

**Important note**

We only got one field back from R, **TransactionAmount**, yet we started our flow with two fields: **Date** and **TransactionAmount**. This is expected behavior; R will only return the fields as specified in its script. In our example script, in the getOutputSchema function, **Date** is not listed and therefore is not returned to Tableau Prep.

It is good practice to avoid sending unnecessary data to R and vice versa, as it could cause performance drawbacks, particularly when working with large datasets. You can always include a unique identifier and join the result from R back to your original dataset.

4.  Change the **Script** step function name from divide to multiply and press
    *Return* again. This time, R will return the TransactionAmount value multiplied
    by 2. This demonstrates that you can have a single R script file with many functions.
    Tableau Prep will only call the function specified in the **Script** step.

    With these steps completed, you've successfully embedded a **Script** step with R in
    your Tableau Prep flow.

## How it works...

In this recipe, we learned how to call an R script and a particular R function from
within the Tableau Prep interface. In doing so, you've opened up the door to integrating
advanced data science methods into your Tableau Prep data preparation process. We've
learned that an R script file may contain multiple functions and that a script step in
Tableau Prep can execute one of those functions by specifying the function name. We also
learned that a function only returns data to Tableau Prep if it includes a specific function,
getOutputSchema, and only the data specified in that function.

# Forecasting time series using R

In the previous two recipes, *Preparing Tableau Prep to work with R* and *Embedding R
code in a Tableau Prep flow*, you learned how to set up **R, RStudio**, and **Rserve**, as well as
integrating an R script into **Tableau Prep**. The example script used was relatively basic and
required no additional configuration. However, R is an extensible programming language,
and many functions are bundled in what are called **packages**. In this recipe, we'll look at
a more advanced script that has dependencies on such packages. You'll learn how to
prepare R for these complex scripts that require additional preparation.

## Getting ready

To follow along with this recipe, download the Sample Files 8.3 folder from this
book's GitHub repository.

---

**Important note**

The R scripts in this book serve to illustrate the process of integrating R
and Tableau Prep. Each dataset must be carefully analyzed prior to applying
advanced functionality such as forecasting. The script referenced in this recipe
is purely for illustration purposes and is not intended for real-world use.

---

# How to do it...

Start by opening up Tableau Prep and connecting to the `Transaction Amount by Date.xlsx` Excel file included in the sample files for this recipe, then follow the steps:

1.  Click the + icon and add a **Script** step. Configure the step to use the `forecast.R` script provided with the resources for this lesson. Set the function name to `forecastTS` and press the *Return* key on your keyboard.

    The **forecastTS** function contains a script that is designed to take time series data and predict, or forecast, future performance. In our case, our sample data contains **Date** and **TransactionAmount**. We'll run the data through this script, which has been designed to forecast the **TransactionAmount** value for the next 30 days (relative to the maximum date in our data):

Figure 8.14 – Configure the Script step for the forecastTS function

You'll notice Tableau Prep will show an error message when it is trying to validate the flow and leverage the specified R function. In this case, the error is caused by the fact that our script depends on extra R packages that we have not installed.

2.  Open up the `forecast.R` script in a text editor. Any time a script requires a package, it will refer to that package as `library(package name)`. In this script, we can see that the script leverages many packages:

```
forecastTS = function(df)
{
    library(dplyr)
    library(zoo)
    library(car)
    library(forecast)
    library(tseries)
    library(fUnitRoots)
    library(PerformanceAnalytics)

    data = df

    Date =as.Date(data$Date,format="%d/%m/%y")
    maxDate=max(as.Date(data$Date,format="%d/%m/%y"))

    #creating ts models
    TS = xts(data$TransactionAmount, order.by = as.Date(data$Date))
    m1=auto.arima(TS)

    #forecasting
    fore = forecast::forecast(m1, h=30)
    ar = as.data.frame(fore)
    sepdf=ar[,c(1,4,5)]
    date=seq(from=maxDate+1,to=maxDate+30,by=1)
    Forecast=cbind(date,sepdf)

    Date=format(date, "%Y-%m-%d")

    Forecast=ar[, 1]
    Low95=ar[,4]
    High95=ar[,5]

    return(data.frame(
    Date,Forecast,Low95,High95
    ))

}

getOutputSchema <- function() {
    return (data.frame(
    Date = prep_date(),
    Forecast = prep_decimal(),
    Low95 = prep_decimal(),
    High95 = prep_decimal()
    ))
}
```

Figure 8.15 – Review the script for package (library) dependencies

3.  Open up RStudio and run the `install.packages("package name")` command from the console. This will cause RStudio to reach out to its online package repository to download the required files and install the package. You can issue multiple commands at the same time. For example, this code block will install all the packages our script needs:

```
install.packages("dplyr")
install.packages("zoo")
install.packages("car")
install.packages("forecast")
install.packages("tseries")
install.packages("fUnitRoots")
install.packages("PerformanceAnalytics")
```

Run the preceding code to install all packages. The following screenshot shows how your RStudio console will appear during this process:

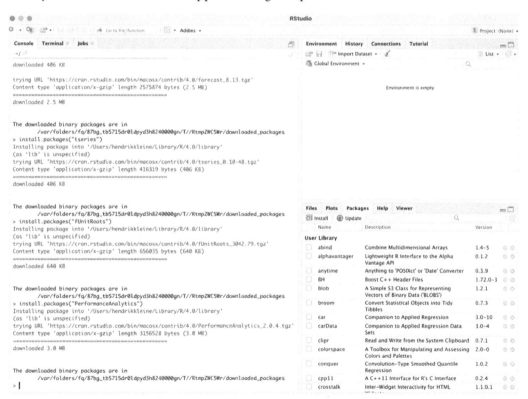

Figure 8.16 – Install missing R packages using RStudio

4.  Return to Tableau Prep and deselect the **Script** step by clicking any white space in the flow diagram. Then, select the **Script** step again. This will prompt Tableau Prep to re-run the script. This time, the script runs successfully and returns the forecast data to Tableau Prep:

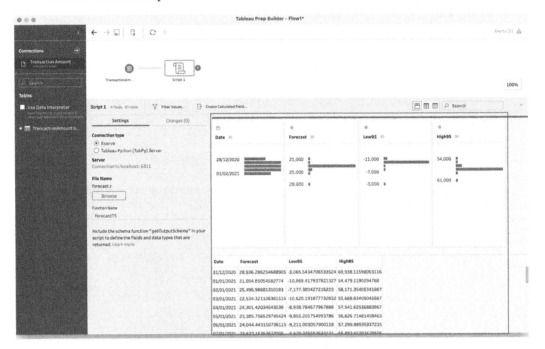

Figure 8.17 – Advanced R script integration returning results to Tableau Prep

> **Important note**
>
> In *Step 4*, notice how the Script step returns more fields than were originally inputted. As highlighted in the previous recipe, titled *Embedding R code in a Tableau Prep flow*, which fields are returned to Tableau Prep is determined by the R script. Since an R script can also generate data and new fields, it is entirely possible for it to output more fields than were inputted. You can always refer back to the **getOutputSchema** function in the R script to evaluate what data is being returned to Tableau Prep.

With these steps completed, you've successfully integrated a complex R script in Tableau Prep.

## How it works...

In this recipe, we learned how to install additional R packages to support complex R scripts. When it comes to R, there is a near-infinite amount of code possibilities driven by a large community of authors. It is good practice to consult your data science teams prior to implementing any R script in your Tableau Prep flow so that you can validate that the script is indeed appropriate for your data.

# Preparing Tableau Prep to work with Python

**Python** is a general-purpose programming language ranking highly as one of the most popular languages right now. It is available free of charge and, similar to R, benefits from a community for ideation and support. To find out more about Python, visit `https://www.python.org/`. In order to allow Tableau Prep to communicate with Python, you need to prepare your machine with a **Tableau Python server** known as **TabPy**.

---

**Important note**

The Python programming language and the TabPy package are not part of Tableau Prep. Python is a separate technology and an in-depth look at Python is beyond the scope of this book. Every system is slightly different, and you may run into unexpected challenges. For help, please refer to the Python website at `https://www.python.org/`.

---

In this recipe, we will provide general guidance for configuring your system successfully.

## Getting ready

If you are a Windows user, you must ensure you have **Microsoft C++ Build Tools** installed. You can download this at `https://visualstudio.microsoft.com/visual-cpp-build-tools/`.

## How to do it...

Start by opening your terminal. On **macOS**, you can find your **Terminal** application in **Applications**, in the **Utilities** folder. On **Windows** machines, use the **Start** menu to search for CMD, then select **Command Prompt** from the search results:

1. We'll first determine the version of Python you are running, if any. To do so, type `python --version` in your terminal and press *Return*:

```
Last login: Tue Jan  5 06:31:29 on ttys000
[hendrikkleine@Hendriks-MBP ~ % python --version
Python 3.9.1
hendrikkleine@Hendriks-MBP ~ %
```

Figure 8.18 – Check your version of Python using the terminal

The terminal will either return a version number or inform you that *Python was not found*. If your version is lower than **3.8**, which is what we are using while writing this book, or you receive the *Python was not found* message, you need to install a newer version of Python. If you have Python 3.8 or higher, you can skip ahead to *Step 5*.

2. To install Python, go to `https://www.python.org/downloads/` and download the latest **3.8.x** version. At the time of writing, this is **3.8.7**.

---

**Important note**

Not all versions of Python will be suitable for running TabPy. We found that the latest version (at the time of writing), 3.9.1, has some challenges with running TabPy. If you are a macOS user, it's important to note that all Macs ship with Python installed. The installation of a newer version may not cause the terminal to actually use that version. That is, you will see the same version number after the installation as you did in *Step 1*. This does not mean the installation has failed, but that your machine has multiple versions of Python installed. There are several ways to adjust this. However, which method you choose is up to you. It's a topic of discussion between Python programmers. You can select a simple solution, as described in this forum article: `https://stackoverflow.com/questions/43354382/how-to-switch-python-versions-in-terminal/`, or you can search online for a so-called Python version manager. As the scope of this book does not cover Python itself, we shall assume that, from *Step 5* onward, you are able to run Python version 3.9.1 or higher from your terminal.

---

3. Install Python. If you are on Windows, ensure you check the **Add Python 3.8 to PATH** box. Accept all other installer defaults and complete the installation:

Figure 8.19 – Check the Add Python to PATH checkbox on Windows

4. Close any terminals you may have open. Then, re-open the terminal and run the `python --version` command to confirm your Python version is the version you just installed.

5. Next, we need to upgrade the Python package manager, `pip`.

> **Important note**
> TabPy installation instructions are documented on TabPy's GitHub repository, which you can find at `https://github.com/tableau/TabPy/blob/master/docs/server-install.md`. Refer to this page if you experience any installation issues and verify the steps you've taken.

In your terminal application, run the `python -m pip install --upgrade pip` command to update `pip`, an installation manager that ships with Python.

6. When done, run the `pip install tabpy` command to install the Tableau Python server, **TabPy**. This may take a few minutes to complete.

7.  Now that we have installed TabPy, we can start it using the terminal. Run the `tabpy` command to start up the Tableau Python server. Within a few moments, the terminal should return a message stating **Web service listening on port 9004**. This indicates your server is running. You can confirm this by opening your browser and navigating to `http://localhost:9004/`, which will display the TabPy server info page:

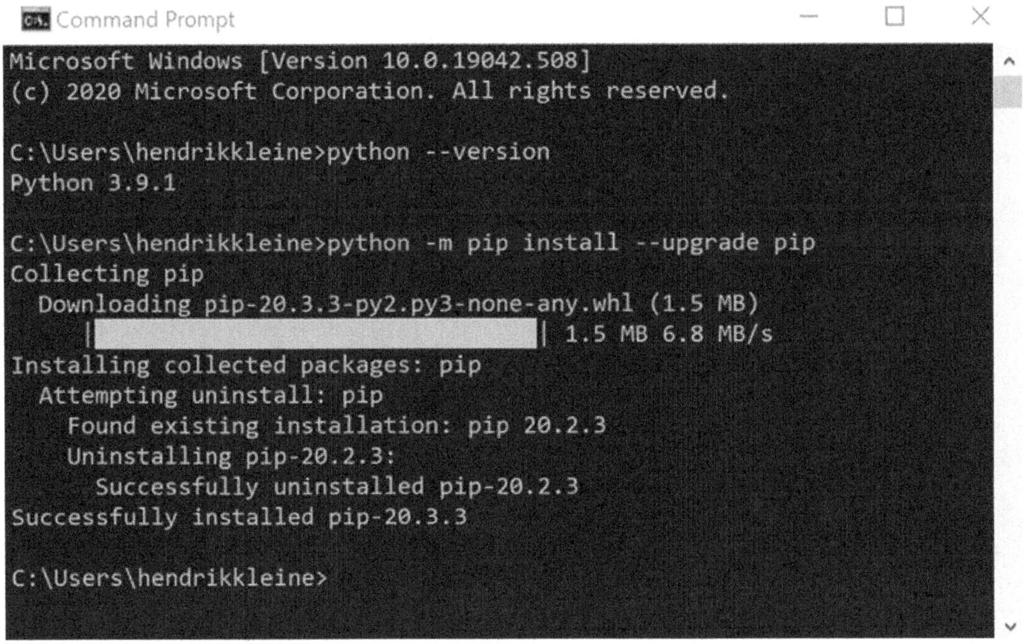

Figure 8.20 – Confirm TabPy is running by browsing to localhost:9004

> **Important note**
>
> Whenever you close all terminal windows or reboot your machine, you will likely shut down the TabPy server. To restart the server, simply open up your terminal and run the `tabpy` command again.

8.  Lastly, we need to configure Tableau Prep to use our new TabPy server. To do this, open up Tableau Prep and select **Manage Analytics Extension Connection** from the **Settings and Performance** section in the **Help** menu.

Set the server name to `localhost` and the port to `9004` and click **Sign In** to save your configuration:

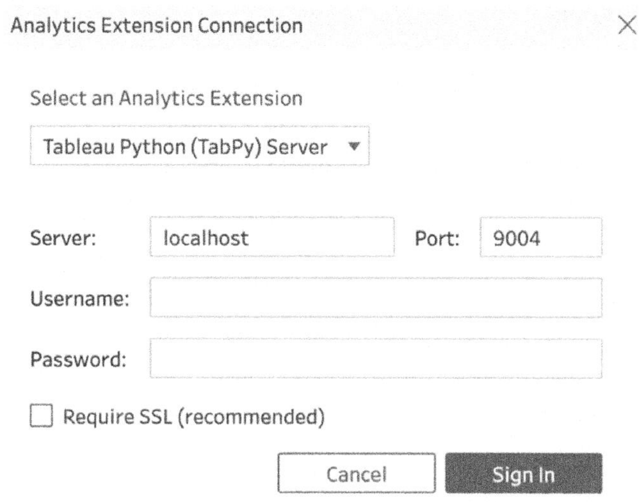

Analytics Extension Connection                                    ✕

Select an Analytics Extension

[ Tableau Python (TabPy) Server    ▼ ]

Server:    [ localhost          ]    Port:    [ 9004     ]

Username:  [                             ]

Password:  [                             ]

☐ Require SSL (recommended)

[ Cancel ]    [ Sign In ]

Figure 8.21 – Configure your Tableau Prep connection to the TabPy server

With these steps completed, you've successfully installed and started the Tableau Python server.

## How it works...

In this recipe, we learned how to install and start the Tableau Python server, also known as TabPy, using the terminal. TabPy will allow Tableau Prep to communicate with Python. Similar to R, Tableau Prep will send data to an external Python process using TabPy, and TabPy will deliver any outputs back to Tableau Prep.

# Embedding Python code in a Tableau Prep flow

In the previous recipe, we prepared our machine to work with Python, using the Tableau Python server. In this recipe, we'll create a Tableau Prep flow and embed a Python script in it. This process is largely the same as we've practiced in the recipes for R. Using this script, we'll evaluate a dataset and flag anomalies, that is, outliers.

# Getting ready

To follow along with this recipe, download the `Sample Files 8.5` folder from this book's GitHub repository.

> **Important note**
>
> The Python scripts in this book serve to illustrate the process of integrating Python and Tableau Prep. Each dataset must be carefully analyzed prior to applying advanced functionality such as anomaly detection. The script referenced in this recipe is purely for illustration purposes and is not intended for real-world use.

# How to do it...

Start by opening up Tableau Prep and connect to the `sales amount by date.csv` file from the sample files folder:

1. Click the + icon on the input step and select **Script** to add an analytic script step to your flow.

2. Configure the **Script** step by setting the connection type to **Tableau Python (TabPy) Server**.

3. Select the `outlier detection.py` file from the sample data folder as the script file.

   This script summarizes time series data by day and then performs analysis to identify outliers, that is, relatively high or low numbers, relative to the entire dataset. You can open up the script in a text editor to look under the hood.

   Similar to R scripts, we must specify a function and DataFrame for Tableau Prep to pass data to, and the script must include the `get_output_schema` function to return data to Tableau Prep. Unlike R, we do not have to install libraries used by our script upfront.

> **Important note**
>
> Tableau provides useful Python resources in its documentation, available at `https://help.tableau.com/current/prep/en-us/prep_scripts_TabPy.htm`.

The following screenshot shows a Python script, with a function named `detect_outliers` for the forecast function, and a function named `get_output_data` to return data to Tableau Prep:

```python
#!/usr/bin/env python
# coding: utf-8

# import libraries

import pandas as pd
import matplotlib.pyplot as plt

from sklearn.preprocessing import StandardScaler
from sklearn.svm import OneClassSVM

# Function
def detect_outliers(input_df, outliers_fraction=0.05):

    # Sorting it by the Date Column
    df = input_df.sort_values('date')

    # Taking Sum of the Amounts on a given day (Remove if unique 'amount' on a given day)
    df = pd.pivot_table(df, index='date', values='amount', aggfunc='sum')
    df = df.reset_index()

    # Scaling the Data
    scaler = StandardScaler()
    scaled_data = scaler.fit_transform(pd.DataFrame(df['amount']))
    data = pd.DataFrame(scaled_data)

    # Training the OneClassSVM
    model = OneClassSVM(nu=outliers_fraction, kernel="rbf", gamma=0.1)
    model.fit(data)

    # Getting the Predicted Outliers
    df['anomaly'] = pd.Series(model.predict(data))

    # Setting the 'anomaly' column as boolean
    df['anomaly'] = [True if x == -1 else False for x in df['anomaly']]

    output_df = input_df

    return df

def get_output_schema():
    return pd.DataFrame({
        'date' : prep_date(),
        'amount' : prep_decimal(),
        'anomaly' : prep_bool()
    })
```

Figure 8.22 – Review the Python script

4. Finally, we need to specify a function name. A script file can have multiple functions and we need to let Tableau Prep know which one to execute. As you can see from *Figure 8.23*, we have just one function, named **detect_outliers**. Set that as the function name:

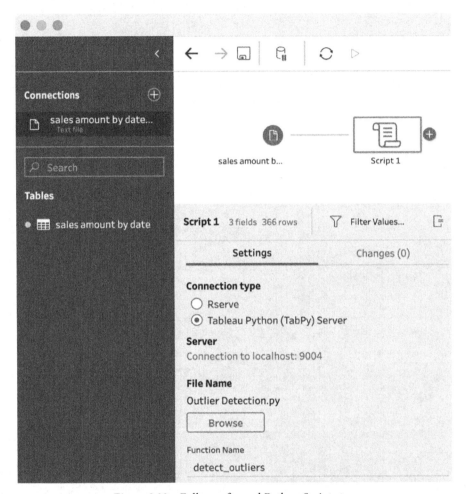

Figure 8.23 – Fully configured Python Script step

5. Press *Return* to complete the configuration. At this time, Tableau Prep will immediately run the **Script** step and after a few moments, you should see the result data. The script will return the source data, aggregated by day, and specify whether or not the value for that day was an outlier in the **anomaly** field.

Scroll through the data and observe the results. We can see that **11/01/2020** has been flagged as an anomaly. Looking at its value of **1,351**, that makes sense as its neighboring values are significantly higher:

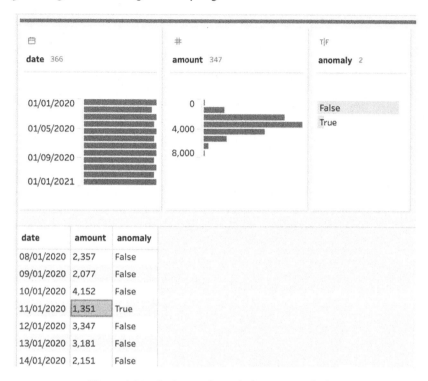

Figure 8.24 – Script results include an anomaly flag

With these steps done, you've successfully completed this recipe.

# How it works...

In this recipe, we learned how to integrate a Python script into a Tableau Prep workflow. Similar to R scripts, a Python script may contain multiple functions, but the **Script** step can only perform the single function specified. The script must include a function named `get_output_data` to return data to Tableau Prep, as we have done in this recipe. This analytics extension can add significant functions to your flow that are not available out of the box.

# 9
# Creating Prep Flows in Various Business Scenarios

So far in this book, we've learned a wide variety of capabilities offered by Tableau Prep. In this chapter, we're going to cover creating an end-to-end flow in Tableau Prep. Each recipe will allow you to prepare for a realistic business scenario in which you may use Tableau Prep. In the first recipe, we'll build a data flow that prepares transaction data for a chain of stores, for the purpose of downstream analysis. During this process, we'll prepare the data and perform cleanup actions so that the downstream analysis can leverage a comprehensive and clean dataset. In the second recipe, we'll use Tableau Prep to answer questions. That is, we'll transform the data to answer a specific business question. Both of these recipes mimic real-world scenarios that you are likely to encounter, no matter the industry you work in.

In this chapter, we will cover the following recipes:

- Creating a flow for transaction analytics
- Creating a call center flow for instant analysis

# Technical requirements

To follow along with the recipes in this chapter, you will require Tableau Prep Builder.

The recipes in this chapter use sample data files that you can download from the book's GitHub repository at `https://github.com/PacktPublishing/Tableau-Prep-Cookbook`.

# Creating a flow for transaction analytics

In this recipe, we'll create a data pipeline, or flow, for analytics. In this scenario, we'll assume that we are an analyst for a fictive department store with multiple physical stores, as well as an online store front. We will be presented with multiple data sources that need to be combined, cleaned, and transformed so that we can output a clean and reliable dataset of all transactions that occurred in the first six months of 2020. This is a common scenario in most industries and is the perfect use case for Tableau Prep.

## Getting ready

To follow along with this recipe, download the `Sample Files 9.1` folder from this book's GitHub repository. In here you'll find various data files. Several of these files originate from disparate systems and we'll need to employ Tableau Prep to provide a single, holistic output of all transactions.

The contents of the files are as follows:

- Files starting with `OnlineSales` contain sales information for transactions made through the company website. There is one file per calendar month, and so we must combine six files to get the full dataset we need for the first six months of 2020.
- `STORE_SALES_EXPORT.xlsx` contains sales data from physical stores. The stores sell the same products as the online storefront. However, the data format is different as the stores use a different point-of-sale system. This data export contains all store sales for the six-month period we need, from January to June 2020.
- `Products.csv` contains descriptive product information, such as the product name and category. We will need to join this to the sales data so that the new dataset is easier to understand, as the sales data only includes product IDs.
- `ShippingData.hyper` is a Tableau Hyper extract prepared by our analyst colleague who works in the shipping department. The data contains product shipping information for those products that were sold online. The company does not provide a delivery service for products bought in their physical stores.
- `CustomerList.csv` contains our customer information for those customers who have created an account with the company. Let's assume that creating a customer account for online transactions is mandatory. However, in-store transactions only have a customer ID if the customer uses their optional loyalty card.

- `returns_h1_2020.csv` contains product return information.

In this recipe, we're going to combine all of these datasets using a number of techniques we've learned in this book. The output of our flow will be a comprehensive dataset that can be easily understood and used for downstream analysis purposes.

## How to do it...

Start by opening up Tableau Prep and connect to the `OnlineSales_2020_01.csv` file from the `Sample Files 9.1` folder in Tableau Prep. Then, perform the following steps:

1. This dataset contains data for a single month. Specifically, the month of January, as indicated by the last two numbers in the filename. The format of all files starting with `OnlineSales` are the same, and so we can combine these files using the **UNION** functionality with the input step. To do this, select the **Multiple Files** tab in the **Input** settings and select **Wildcard union**. Then, set the matching pattern to **OnlineSales\***. This will instruct Tableau Prep to union all files starting with `OnlineSales`. Make sure to click **Applied** to save your settings:

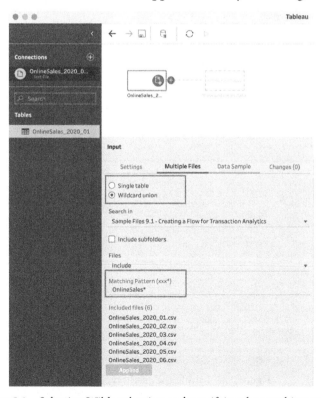

Figure 9.1 – Selecting Wildcard union and specifying the matching pattern

2.  As a result of our union action, Tableau Prep has automatically added the **File Paths** field, to indicate where each row of data originated. As we won't require this information for any type of analysis, we can remove it here simply by unchecking the box in the field list:

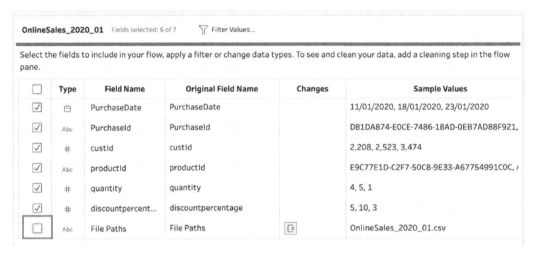

Figure 9.2 – Deselecting the File Paths field

3.  Observe the field list and note how Tableau Prep has wrongly assigned a numeric data type to the **custId** field. This field represents the customer ID and although it consists of numbers, it will not be used as such in any calculation. Correct the data type by clicking the data type icon **#** and select **String** instead:

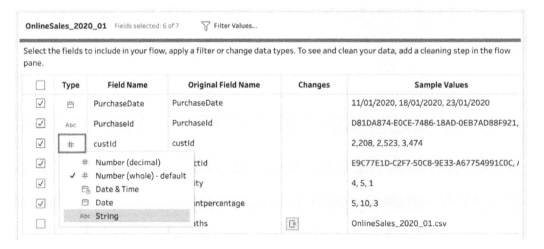

Figure 9.3 – Setting the custId type to String

4.  Next, let's add the sales data for our physical stores. Use the Connect to Excel functionality and select the STORE_SALES_EXPORT.xlsx file provided in the sample files folder. Unlike the online sales data we have worked with so far, this dataset contains data for the full 6 months, so we don't have to perform a union here.

5.  With the new input selected, correct the data type for the **TransactionID** and **CustomerID** fields by changing the type to **String**. This is the same solution we applied in *Step 3*, and something that occurs frequently in real-world scenarios when your data contains numeric IDs.

6.  Before we continue, let's name the steps in our flow. As we'll build out a relatively large flow, naming your steps is useful for ensuring that your flow remains easy to understand. Rename the OnlineSales_2020_01 input step by double-clicking its name and changing the name to Online Sales. Then, rename the second dataset to In-Store Sales:

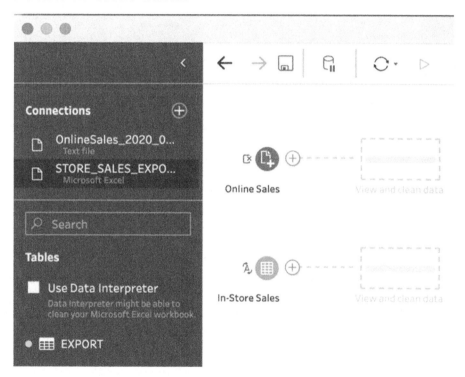

Figure 9.4 – Double-clicking the inputs to rename them

7.  Click the + icon besides the **In-Store Sales** input and then select **Clean Step**. Observe the **TransactionDate** field values, as highlighted in the following screenshot. Each value here seems to be a number and not a date. This is because the input data has been formatted as a **UNIX TIMESTAMP**. This type of data issue is not uncommon, and we need to create a simple calculated field to convert this value to a date, as Tableau Prep cannot automatically convert this source field to a date:

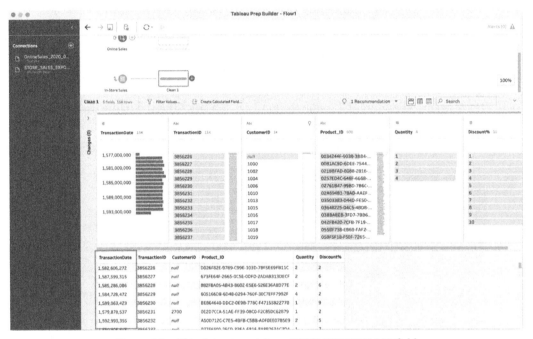

Figure 9.5 – This dataset contains a UNIX TIMESTAMP field

8.  With **Clean Step** still selected, click on **Create Calculated Field…**. Name the new field `Purchase Date` and set the expression to `DATEADD('second',[TransactionDate],#1970-01-01#)`, which is the expression to convert a Unix timestamp to a regular datetime format. Click **Save** when done to apply your new calculation:

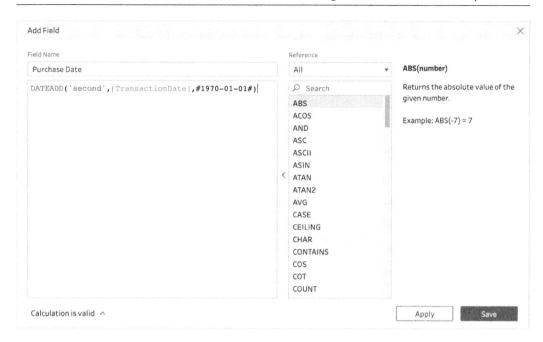

Figure 9.6 – Calculating the date value

Observe the outcome and ensure that the format is indeed date and time, as shown in the following screenshot:

| Purchase Date | TransactionDate |
|---|---|
| 25/02/2020, 04:51:12 | 1,582,606,272 |
| 22/04/2020, 23:48:35 | 1,587,599,315 |
| 27/03/2020, 05:14:46 | 1,585,286,086 |
| 20/03/2020, 18:21:12 | 1,584,728,472 |
| 09/05/2020, 22:30:23 | 1,589,063,423 |
| 24/01/2020, 15:08:57 | 1,579,878,537 |
| 24/06/2020, 10:09:15 | 1,592,993,355 |

Figure 9.7 – The result of converting the Unix timestamp

9.  We won't need the specific time for the purchase date, so let's change the data type from **Date & Time** to **Date** by clicking the data type icon in the field list and then selecting **Date**, as shown in the following screenshot:

Figure 9.8 – Using the icon dropdown to change the data type to Date

10. We also no longer require the original **TransactionDate** field. To remove this field using the clean step, click the context menu next to the field name and then select **Remove**, as shown in the following screenshot:

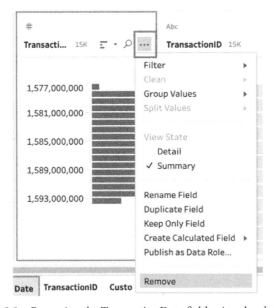

Figure 9.9 – Removing the TransactionDate field using the clean step

11. Next, we're going to combine the online sales data with our in-store sales data. To do this, we need to perform a union. Drag and hover **Clean Step** on top of the **Online Sales** input. Then, from the options that appear, hover over **Union** and release, as shown in the following screenshot:

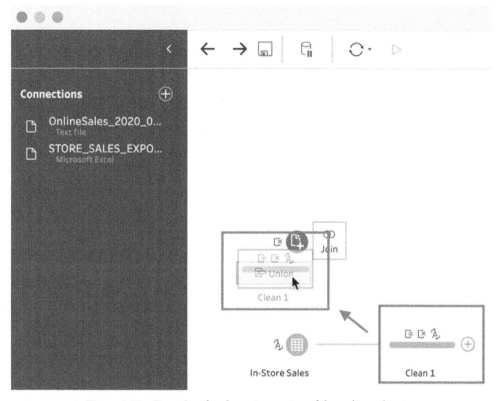

Figure 9.10 – Dragging the clean step on top of the online sales step

This will automatically create a **Union** step and your screen should look like the following screenshot:

Figure 9.11 – A Union step has been added as a result of the drag and drop action

12. In the bottom left of the window, we can see that there are quite a few **Mismatched Fields** options. This is to be expected when you combine data from different sources, as we have just done. Fortunately, both our sources include fields with a similar meaning and they just have different field names, which prevents Tableau Prep from automatically aligning them. To resolve this, click the field pairs that represent the same information (hold the *Command* or *CTRL* key to select the second field), and then right-click and select **Merge Fields**, as shown in the following screenshot for the **Purchase Date** and **PurchaseDate** fields. Note that the newly merged field will take the name of the field you right-clicked:

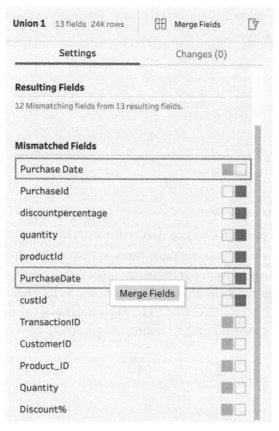

Figure 9.12 – Right-clicking and select Merge Fields to merge the selected fields

Perform this **Merge Fields** action for the field pairs listed here:

- **Purchase Date** and **PurchaseDate**
- **PurchaseId** and **TransactionID**
- **discountpercentage** and **Discount%**
- **quantity** and **Quantity**
- **productId** and **Product_ID**
- **custId** and **CustomerID**

When you've completed all the merges, your **Settings** tab should look like the following screenshot:

Figure 9.13 – The Resulting Fields section is empty when all mismatches have been merged

13. With the **Union** step still selected, notice that a new field has appeared in the **Union Results** field list, named **Table Names**. This field indicates where each row originated, that is, from our online sales dataset or the in-store dataset. This field may come in handy for downstream analysis, so let's rename the value STORE_SALES_EXPORT.xlsx/EXPORT to **In-Store Sales** and the field name itself to Sales Type, as shown in the following screenshot:

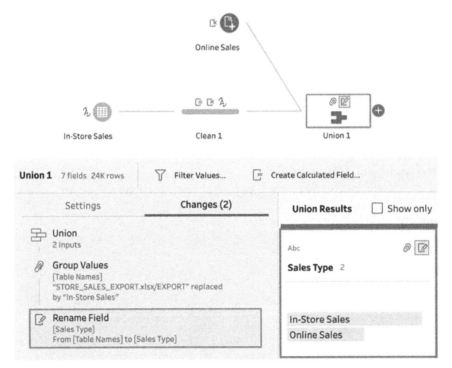

Figure 9.14 – Renaming the value and field name for the automatically added Table Names field

14. Next, create another data connection, this time to the `Products.csv` file, provided in the sample files with this lesson.

15. This `Products.csv` file we just added contains descriptive product information. For example, instead of using a product ID such as *1931E212-FF85-3A36-620A-8C56D1C6B605*, we can get a name such as *Modern Utility Laptop Messenger Bag*. To add this information to our existing dataset as additional columns, we need to perform a join. To do this, drag the input on top of the **Union** step. When the **Union** and **Join** options appear, drop the input on top of the **Join** option to instantly add a join step.

16. Configure the join by specifying a common field between the two datasets, in this case, **productId** and **ID**, as shown in the following screenshot. The default join type, inner, can be left as-is:

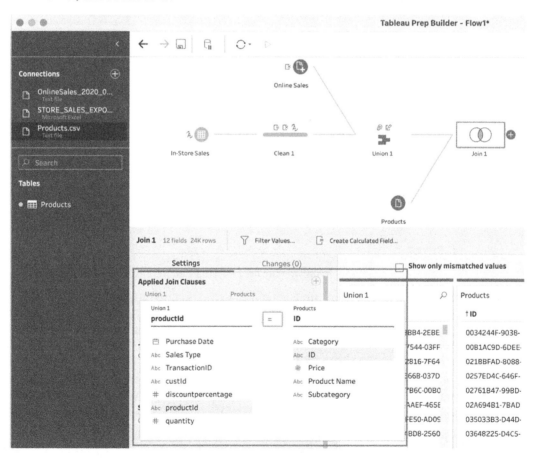

Figure 9.15 – Configuring the join to join on the productId and ID fields

17. As is typical with a join, we now have a redundant field for product ID. Remove the **ID** field from the field list by selecting **Remove** from the field context menu. This way, we only have the **productId** field as the identifier:

Figure 9.16 – Removing the field ID from Join Results

18. Add another data source, this time a Tableau extract named `ShippingData.hyper`. This data is provided by our shipping department and contains shipping information for sales completed online. Rename the step `Shipping`.

19. Add a clean step to the **Shipping** input and observe the field named **ID**. The shipping ID here is made up of two identifiers; first, the shipping department's ID, followed by an underscore symbol and then the purchase ID. We need to split this field so that these values are stored separately. To do this, select **Custom Split…** from the context menu for the **ID** field:

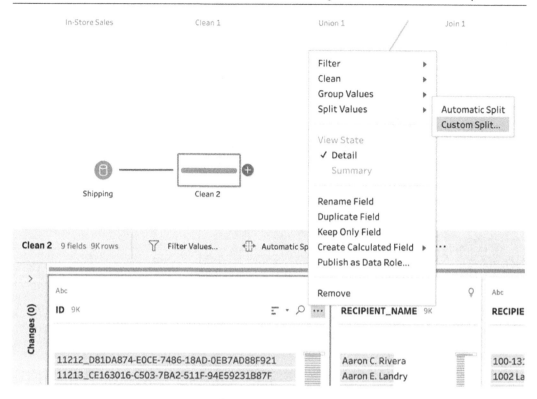

Figure 9.17 – Selecting Custom Split for the ID field

- Configure the split to use the underscore (_) symbol as a separator and split the first **2** fields, as shown in the following screenshot:

Figure 9.18 – Configuring Custom Split with an underscore and the first 2 fields

- When you're ready, click **Split**. This will then split the ID field into two new fields, named **ID - Split 1** and **ID - Split 2**:

20. Rename the **ID - Split 1** field to `Shipping ID` and the **ID - Split 2** field to `Purchase ID`.

21. We will no longer need the original **ID** field, so use the context menu to remove it from the dataset.

22. Drop the **Shipping** input on top of the existing join in order to create another **Join** step. Configure the join clause to use the **TransactionID** and **Purchase ID** fields to perform the join. Because only sales are shipped, the shipping data does not contain information for store sales. As such, we need to set this join to a left join type. A left join will result in including all data from the left dataset, which is our main flow, and any matching data from the right dataset, which is our shipping data. Set **Join Type** to **left** by selecting the left circle in the Venn diagram. Your flow and join settings should look like those in the following screenshot:

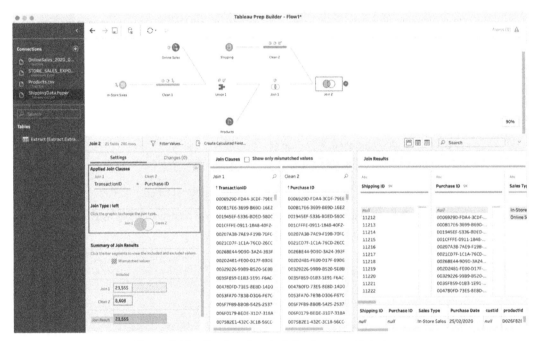

Figure 9.19 – Configuring the join clause and join type

23. Delete the now redundant **Purchase ID** field. We still have the **TransactionID** field to identify a given row of data.

24. Add your fifth data connection to this flow. This time, select the `CustomerList.csv` text file. This input contains information about our customers, such as their full name. Rename the input step to `Customers`.

25. The **Customers** data includes an **ID** field, which has been incorrectly set to a numeric format by Tableau Prep. Click the data type icon for the **ID** field and change the type to **String**.

26. Join the **Customers** data to the existing flow by dropping it on the **Join 2** step. Configure the join clause to join on the **custId** and **id** fields. Because in-store checkouts do not always involve a customer loyalty card, the customer ID is not always known. Given the missing customer IDs, set the join type to **left** using the Venn diagram so that all rows are included from our main flow, including those for which we do not have customer details.

27. Delete the redundant customer ID field, named **id**, which originated from the **Customers** data.

28. Add our final data connection, the text file named `returns_h1_2020.csv`, and rename the step to `Returns`.

29. Correct the data type for the **return_id** field by setting it to **String**.

30. Rename the **status** field to `Return Status` so that we don't mix it up later with the existing status fields from the **Shipping** and **Customer** data.

31. Join the **Returns** step with the main flow by dropping it on top of **Join 3** to create a new join. Configure the join clause to use the **TransactionID** and **purchase_id** fields. Once more, use the Venn diagram to set the join type to **left**. Not all customers are returns, so we want to return all transactions and any matched rows from the **Returns** dataset.

32. Remove the redundant **purchase_id** field from the dataset.

33. Click the + icon on the last join and add a **Clean** step. Using the **Clean** step, rename the fields as follows:

- **custId** to `Customer ID`
- **productId** to `Product ID`
- **quantity** to `Quantity`
- **discountpercentage** to `Discount %`
- **TransactionID** to `Transaction ID`
- **RECIPIENT_NAME** to `Recipient Name`
- **RECIPIENT_STREET** to `Recipient Street`
- **RECIPIENT_CITY** to `Recipient City`

- **RECIPIENT_POSTAL** to `Recipient Postal`
- **RECIPIENT_REGION** to `Recipient Region`
- **SHIPMODE** to `Shipping Mode`
- **TRACEID** to `Shipping Courier Tracking ID`
- **STATUS** to `Shipping Status`
- **name** to `Customer Name`
- **surname** to `Customer Surname`
- **status** to `Customer Membership Status`
- **return_id** to `Return ID`

34. As a final step, we need to add an output step to our flow. Click the + icon on the **Clean** step and select **Output**. Configure the output to write to a location of your choosing and set the filename to `2020-H1 Sales Data.csv` and the **Output** type to **CSV**. Your final flow should look like the following screenshot:

Figure 9.20 – Your completed sales flow

With these steps completed, you've finished this recipe and successfully created a comprehensive sales flow. If you wish, you can run the flow and analyze your data further in an application such as **Tableau Desktop**.

## How it works...

In this recipe, we learned to combine multiple different tools and functions in Tableau Prep to create a comprehensive flow that provides a clean data output that can be used for downstream analysis. We leveraged different methods of input, cleaning, pivoting, union, join, calculated fields, and aggregation to create the ideal dataset and even perform quick analysis in Tableau Prep. This combination of tools is very common in flows and offers significant added value to companies who want to combine data from disparate systems into a single, holistic view.

# Creating a call center flow for instant analysis

In this recipe, we'll explore another typical real-world example. In the previous recipe, *Creating a flow for transaction analytics*, our focus was to provide a new data *output* that could be used for further analytical purposes. In contrast, in this recipe, we'll leverage Tableau Prep to investigate data in order to answer a business question. That is, our objective is to find the answer using Tableau Prep itself. You're likely to find similar use cases in any industry, where your leadership relies on you not only preparing data but investigating that data and elaborating on things such as business performance using key metrics or performing a deep dive analysis for a specific scenario.

## Getting ready

To follow along with this recipe, download the `Sample Files 9.2` folder from this book's GitHub repository. The files here contain information from a call center for a company selling laptops and desktop PCs. There are data files included for the month of January 2021 that include call information, case data from a CRM system, and an extract from a **Customer Satisfaction** (**CSAT**) survey. The CSAT survey is an optional survey sent to customers following a call and asks them to rate their satisfaction with the interaction on a scale of 1 to 10, where 1 is very dissatisfied and 10 is very satisfied. Let's assume that recently, the **Customer Satisfaction Score**, also known as the **CSAT Score**, has decreased and your leadership has tasked you with investigating why that may be. Using Tableau Prep, we're going to investigate the data available in order to identify some clues as to what may be affecting the drop in CSAT.

# How to do it...

Let's start looking at the customer satisfaction data. Open a new Tableau Prep instance and connect to the `csat_data.csv` file from the `Sample Files 9.2` folder. Then, perform the following steps:

1. Start off by correcting the data types. Change **survey_id** to **String** and amend **call_id** to **String** as well:

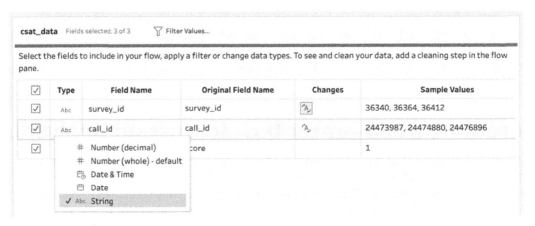

Figure 9.21 – Set the survey_id and call_id field types to String

2. Next, click the + icon and add a **Clean** step to your flow. Observe the data profile and you will notice that the distribution of the survey score is skewed toward the lower end, as shown in the following screenshot. This is expected as we're investigating the reason behind the business's low survey score:

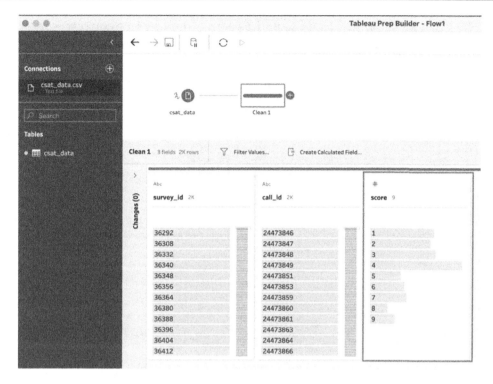

Figure 9.22 – Using a Clean step to quickly view the data profile for the score field

3.  Let's now get the average score by adding an **Aggregate** step. In the step configuration, drag and drop the **score** field to the **Aggregated Fields** section, and click **SUM**, followed by **Average**, to get the average score across all surveys. Here, we can see that our average score is 4.05, as shown in the following screenshot:

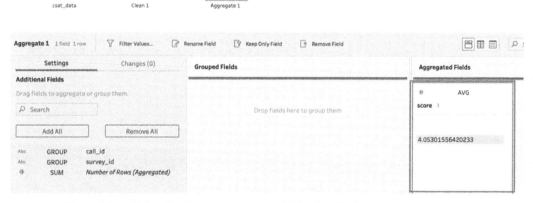

Figure 9.23 – Using the Aggregate step to quickly identify the average survey score

4.  Now that we know the average score, let's narrow our dataset to surveys where the customer scored between 1 and 4. To do this, select the **Clean** step, select the score values **1**, **2**, **3**, and **4** (use the *Command* or *CTRL* key to multi-select), and then right-click and select **Keep Only**. This will filter our survey data for scores 1-4 only:

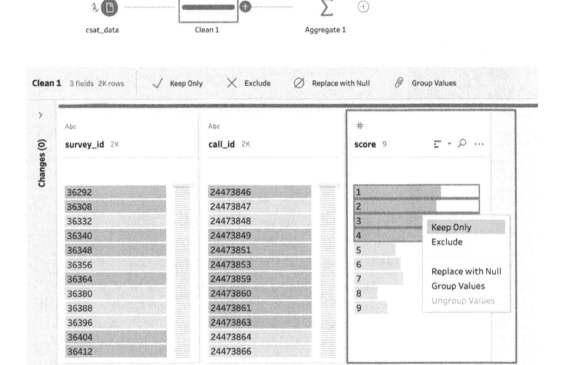

Figure 9.24 – Using the Clean step to filter survey data for scores 1-4 only

5.   Let's see what we can find out from the call data for these surveys. Add another data connection, this time to the file `call_data.csv`. This dataset contains information about the date the call was made, how long the customer had to wait before being connected to a customer service agent (the **wait_time_seconds** field), the duration of the conversation with the agent (**call_time_seconds**), and the time the agent spent updating the case management system after the call ended (**after_call_seconds**). Before you continue, correct the **call_id** field data type by setting it to **String**, as shown in the following screenshot:

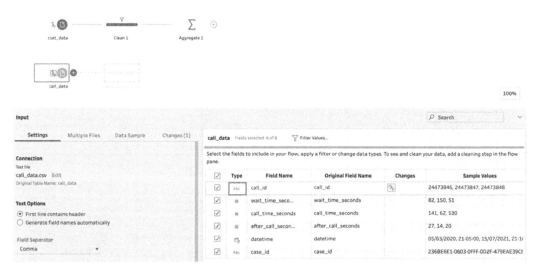

Figure 9.25 – Correcting the call_id type in the newly added call_data connection field

6.  Let's join this data with our survey data. To do this, drag the **call_data** step on top
    of the **Clean** step and select **Join** to instantly add the **Join** step. Notice how Tableau
    Prep seamlessly branches our flow (the original branch ending with **Aggregate**), as
    shown in the following screenshot. Since our two datasets contain the same field
    name, **call_id**, Tableau Prep automatically configures **Join Clauses** to use that field,
    which is appropriate. We can leave the **Join Type** default set to **Inner**, which ensures
    that only calls matching our filtered survey data come through:

Figure 9.26 – Joining call_data with the Clean step to create a new branch in your flow

7.  To keep your dataset lean, add a new **Clean** step after **Join** and remove the duplicate field, **call_id-1**.

8.  Let's pull up the average call times next. Add a new **Aggregate** step after **Join** and drag the **wait_time_seconds**, **call_time_seconds**, and **after_call_seconds** fields to the **Aggregated Fields** section and change the aggregate for all fields from **SUM** to **Average**. In order to easily view the results, add a **Clean** step after **Aggregate**, as shown in the following screenshot:

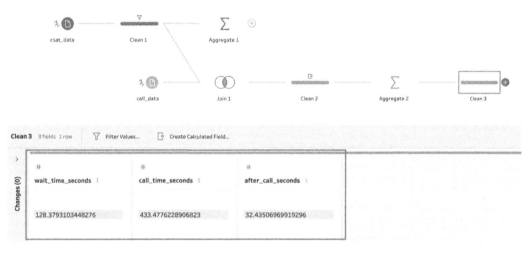

Figure 9.27 – Adding Aggregate and Clean steps to view average call time information

We will need to compare this information to calls with a higher survey score, that is, calls with a score of between 5 and 10. We'll proceed to do so in the next step.

9.  Go ahead and, once again, join the **call_data** field with the first **Clean** step, resulting
    in a third branch in our flow. This time, we are only interested in calls where the
    user had either no survey score at all (which is possible, because the survey is
    optional), or a score higher than 4. To do this, configure **Join Type** to **rightOnly**
    using the Venn diagram illustration. This will result in returning all data from the
    right side, which is the call data that does not match any data in the filtered clean
    step (which is filtered for results with a score of 1-4 only):

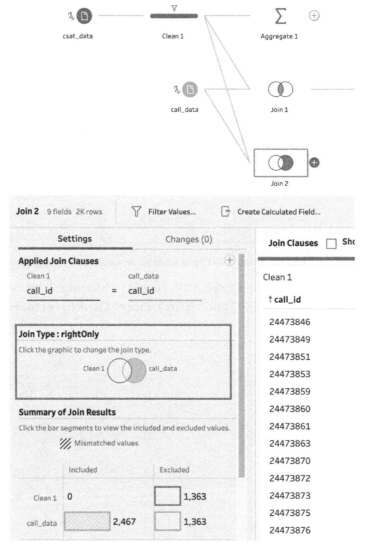

Figure 9.28 – Configuring the new join to Join Type : rightOnly

10. To keep our data tidy, add a **Clean** step and remove the duplicate **call_id** field, keeping **call_id-1**.

> **Important note**
>
> In this exercise, we're using the Clean step function to remove fields from the dataset that have become redundant following a Join step. It should be noted that the same action, removing a field, can be performed in the Join step itself, even if that field is part of the Join clause. It's a personal preference related to how you wish to visually organize your flow.

11. Now that our new, third branch only contains positive survey data (assuming positive is no score, or a score of between 5-10), let's perform the same aggregate analysis we did previously, that is, add a new **Aggregate** step after **Join** and drag the **wait_time_seconds**, **call_time_seconds**, and **after_call_seconds** fields to the **Aggregated Fields** section, and then change the aggregate for all fields from **SUM** to **Average**.

12. To easily compare this result with our previous aggregate result for negative survey call data, drag the step marked **Aggregate 3** on top of **Aggregate 2** and select **Union** to add a **Union** step. In the **Union** step, double-click the **csat_data.csv,call_data.csv** value in the table names field and rename it `Regular/Positive Survey Score`. Then, rename the **call_data.csv-1,csat_data.csv-1** value to `Negative Survey Score`, as shown in the following screenshot:

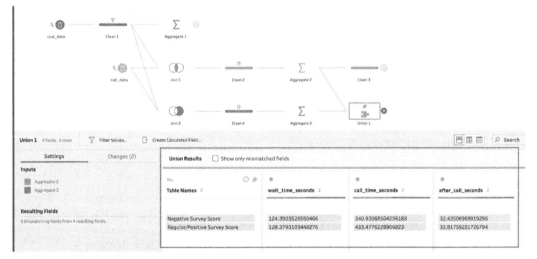

Figure 9.29 – Renaming the values in the automatically added Table Names field

In the **Union Results** view, we can now easily compare the call data. While the **wait_time_seconds** and **after_call_seconds** values are relatively similar, we can see a significant difference in **call_time_seconds**. In fact, it's roughly **27%** (433/349) higher than calls that resulted in a positive feedback score.

13. It might be interesting to see what percentage of callers experienced this higher call time and left a negative score. We can easily go back to any step in our flow and make changes to their configurations, something that is very typical in an ad hoc analysis such as this. Return to both the **Aggregate 2** and **Aggregate 3** steps and add the **Number of Rows** field to the **Aggregated Fields** section. The **Number of Rows** field is automatically generated in the aggregate step and lets us know the row count for the step. When done, return to the **Union** step, as shown in the following screenshot:

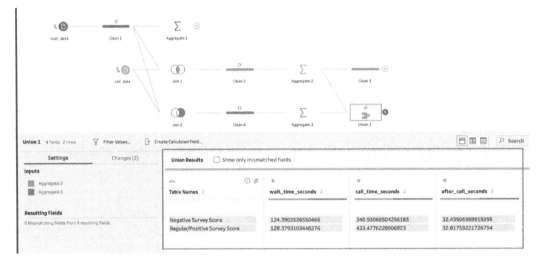

Figure 9.30 – Renaming the values automatically

Notice that **1,363** customers out of a total of 3,830 (**1,363**+**2,467**) customers experienced a higher call time, at least on average, and left a negative survey score. That equates to 36% of all callers.

> **Important note**
> Don't forget your plain old calculator. Oftentimes, simple quick calculations during an ad hoc analysis, such as determining the percentage difference in this step, are done faster on a simple calculator. If you do not need to recalculate this value again or do not intend to run your flow against new data, this simple tip can often save you time.

14. The datasets supplied also include a case data file. This data contains an extract from the call center case management system and records the purpose of the call, as well as the related product. Add a third data connection to your flow for the Excel file, `case_data.xlsx`. In the connection settings, correct the data type for the **call_id** field to **String**.

15. Join the newly added case data with the **Clean 2** step by dragging and dropping the **Case Data** step on top of the **Clean 2** step. The **Clean 2** step contains all the data we have used so far for customers who left a rating of between 1 and 4. By joining it with the case data, we can start identifying the reasons these customers called in. Leave the automatically detected **Join Clause** set to **case_id** and **Join Type** as **inner**, as shown in the following screenshot:

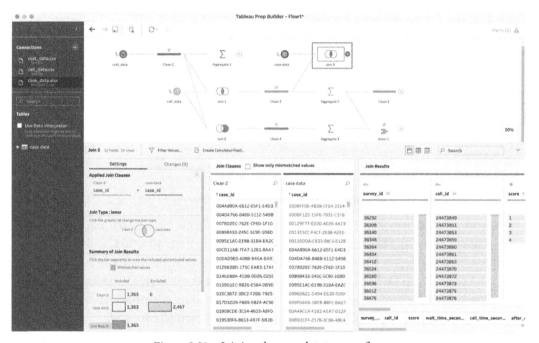

Figure 9.31 – Joining the case data to your flow

16. Add an **Aggregate** step after the newly added **Join 3** and then add **contact_reason** to the **Grouped Fields** section, and **Number of Rows** to the **Aggregated Fields** section, as shown in the following screenshot:

Figure 9.32 – Configuring the Aggregate step to group by the contact_reason field

17. Next, add a **Clean** step and observe the number of rows by **contact_reason**. It's quite obvious that three numbers stand out from the rest: **403**, **404**, and **410** are significantly higher than the other row counts. Select the three numbers, right-click, and select **Keep Only** to filter the data to just these three values. In doing so, we quickly see the three main reasons why people called in: **Firmware Issue**, **Unable to Boot Up**, and **Update Issue**, as shown in the following screenshot:

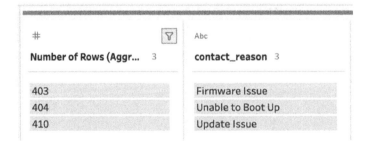

Figure 9.33 – Configuring the Aggregate step

18. To ascertain the percentage of calls routed to these three reasons, click the **Join 3** step to see the number of rows in this branch listed under **Join Result** in the configuration. The number of rows here, **1,363**, is the number of surveys with a score of 4 or lower. With the information collected in *Step 17*, we can calculate the percentage of calls within this subset that are related to one of the three key categories, that is, (403+404+410)/1363 = 89%.

19. `case data` also includes the `product` per case. Let's see which products are affected by the three case reasons we've identified in *Step 17*. To do this, join **Join 3** with **Clean 5**. Leave the default configurations set, with **Join Clause** on **contact_reason** and **Join Type inner**.

20. Finally, add a **Clean** step after the newly added join and remove all fields with the exception of **Number of Rows**, **product**, and **contact_reason**. Now we can clearly see the affected products in the product file, as shown in the following screenshot:

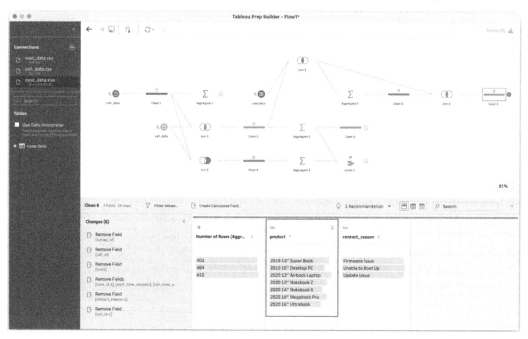

Figure 9.34 – Identifying the products related to the three main contact reasons

With these steps completed, you've successfully performed an ad hoc analysis in Tableau Prep itself. We could summarize our findings in a report to the requestor as follows:

- The average customer satisfaction score for January 2021 is **4.05** (out of 10).

- More than a third, **36%**, of customers rated their level of satisfaction as 4 or lower.

- On average, customers who left negative feedback typically experienced call times **27% longer** compared to call times for customers who left positive feedback.

- Out of **1,363** calls related to negative feedback (4 or lower), **1,217 (89%)** were related to issues with regard to **Firmware, Updates or Booting up**. The products that these calls and issues relate to are the following:

2019 13" Super Book

2019 15" Desktop PC

2020 13" Airbook Laptop

2020 13" Notebook Z

2020 14" Notebook X

2020 16" Megabook Pro

2020 16" Ultrabook

Let's move on to the next section!

## How it works...

In this recipe, we learned to use Tableau Prep as a data investigation tool. We were presented with data and a business question, and we merged different data sources and tools in order to find the answer. This use case presents the incredible value Tableau Prep has to offer as a data analysis tool in its own right. Oftentimes, it can be faster to perform analysis like we did in this recipe, in Tableau Prep itself, rather than performing the additional steps of writing outputs and then continuing the work in a visualization tool.

Packt.com

Subscribe to our online digital library for full access to over 7,000 books and videos, as well as industry leading tools to help you plan your personal development and advance your career. For more information, please visit our website.

## Why subscribe?

- Spend less time learning and more time coding with practical eBooks and Videos from over 4,000 industry professionals

- Improve your learning with Skill Plans built especially for you

- Get a free eBook or video every month

- Fully searchable for easy access to vital information

- Copy and paste, print, and bookmark content

Did you know that Packt offers eBook versions of every book published, with PDF and ePub files available? You can upgrade to the eBook version at packt.com and as a print book customer, you are entitled to a discount on the eBook copy. Get in touch with us at customercare@packtpub.com for more details.

At www.packt.com, you can also read a collection of free technical articles, sign up for a range of free newsletters, and receive exclusive discounts and offers on Packt books and eBooks.

# Other Books You May Enjoy

If you enjoyed this book, you may be interested in these other books by Packt:

**Learning Tableau 2020 - Fourth Edition**

Joshua Milligan

ISBN: 978-1-80020-036-4

- Develop stunning visualizations to explain complex data with clarity
- Explore exciting new Data Model capabilities
- Connect to various data sources to bring all your data together
- Leverage Tableau Prep Builder's amazing capabilities for data cleaning and structuring
- Create and use calculations to solve problems and enrich the analytics

**Tableau Desktop Certified Associate: Exam Guide**

Dmitry Anoshin, Jean-Charles (JC) Gillet, Fabian Peri's, Radhika Biyani, Gleb Makarenko

ISBN: 978-1-83898-413-7

- Acquire the key skills of ethical hacking to perform penetration testing
- Apply Tableau best practices to analyze and visualize data
- Use Tableau to visualize geographic data using vector maps
- Create charts to gain productive insights into data and make quality-driven decisions
- Implement advanced analytics techniques to identify and forecast key values
- Prepare customized table calculations to compute specific values
- Answer questions based on the Tableau Desktop Certified Associate exam with the help of mock tests

# Packt is searching for authors like you

If you're interested in becoming an author for Packt, please visit `authors.packtpub.com` and apply today. We have worked with thousands of developers and tech professionals, just like you, to help them share their insight with the global tech community. You can make a general application, apply for a specific hot topic that we are recruiting an author for, or submit your own idea.

# Leave a review - let other readers know what you think

Please share your thoughts on this book with others by leaving a review on the site that you bought it from. If you purchased the book from Amazon, please leave us an honest review on this book's Amazon page. This is vital so that other potential readers can see and use your unbiased opinion to make purchasing decisions, we can understand what our customers think about our products, and our authors can see your feedback on the title that they have worked with Packt to create. It will only take a few minutes of your time, but is valuable to other potential customers, our authors, and Packt. Thank you!

# Index

## S

SAS (.sas7bdat) files
   connecting to 36-38
Snowflake 53
SPSS (.sav) files
   connecting to 36-38
SQL Server 53
substrings
   extracting 188-194
   working 194

## T

Tableau Data Extract (.tde) 45
Tableau Desktop 251
Tableau Desktop ad hoc analysis
   data, preparing for 20-22
Tableau extracts
   connecting to 45, 46
text files
   connecting to 24-33
Tableau Hyper Extract (.hyper) 45
Tableau Online 91
Tableau Prep
   about 4, 206
   preparing, to work with Python 223-227
   preparing, to work with R 206-214
   using, for ad hoc data analysis 12-16
Tableau Prep Builder
   installing 2-4
   working 4
Tableau Prep flow
   Python code, embedding in 227-231
   R code, embedding in 214-218
Tableau Prep UI
   Athena web interface,
      mapping between 45

Tableau Server
   about 51, 91
   flow, publishing to 61-68
TabPy 223
Teradata 53
time series
   forecasting, with R 218-223
transaction analytics
   flow, creating for 234-251

## U

UNION
   data, combining with 122-129
UNION actions
   combining, with data ingest 129-135
UNION functionality 235
UNIX TIMESTAMP 238
user interface
   checking out 4-12
   working 12

## V

values
   aggregating 109-112
values, grouping in Tableau
      Prep algorithms
   about 120
   common characters 120
   pronunciation 120
   spelling 120

## W

wildcards
   used, for pivoting columns
      to rows 159-163

Made in the USA
Columbia, SC
27 February 2022